Figuring Foreigners Out

Craig Storti is available as a trainer/consultant in the subjects
covered in this book. He can be reached at
e-mail: cstorti@carr.org
Phone: 410-346-7336
Fax: 410-346-7846

Craig Storti is also the author of
Americans at Work: A Guide to the Can-Do People
The Art of Coming Home
The Art of Crossing Cultures
Cross-Cultural Dialogues: 74 Brief Encounters with Cultural Difference
Incident at Bitter Creek
Old World/New World— Bridging Cultural Differences: Britain, France, Germany and the U.S.

Figuring Foreigners Out

A Practical Guide

Craig Storti

INTERCULTURAL PRESS
A Nicholas Brealey Publishing Company

BOSTON • LONDON

First published by Intercultural Press, a Nicholas Brealey
Publishing Company, in 1999. For information contact:

Intercultural Press   Nicholas Brealey Publishing
a division of   3-5 Spafield Street
Nicholas Brealey Publishing   Clerkenwell
20 Park Plaza, Suite 1115A   London EC1R 4QB, UK
Boston, MA 02116, USA   Tel: +44-207-239-0360
Information: 617-523-3801   Fax: +44-207-239-0370
Fax: 617-523-3708   www.nicholasbrealey.com
www.interculturalpress.com

© 1999 by Craig Storti

ISBN-13: 978-1-877864-70-4
ISBN-10: 1-877864-70-6

Printed in the United States of America

15 14 13 12   13 14 15 16

Library of Congress Cataloging-in-Publication Data

Storti, Craig
    Figuring foreigners out: a practical guide/Craig Storti.
        p.   cm.
    Includes bibliographical references.
    ISBN 1-877864-70-6
    1. Cross-cultural orientation. 2. Intercultural
communication. I. Title
GN345.65.S76   1998
303.48'2—dc21   98–40639
                                                        CIP

Dedication

for Charlotte

Table of Contents

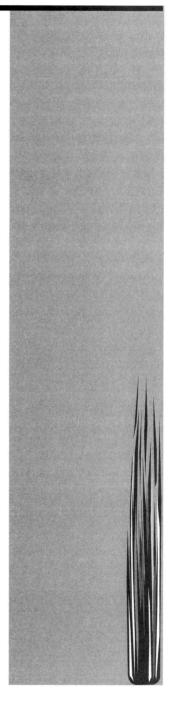

Acknowledgments

In writing this book, I have drawn upon the work of a number of distinguished interculturalists. While I have cited these individuals at appropriate points in the text, I would also like to mention them here. They include Edward Hall, Geert Hofstede, Alfred Kraemer, Fons Trompenaars, Charles Hampden-Turner, and Harry Triandis. It may be that the concepts I have associated with these men herein have in fact been further developed or expanded upon by other individuals of whom I am not aware and whom I have not cited. I do, of course, regret any such omissions.

I also want to add my customary—but no less heartfelt—appreciation to David and Kathleen Hoopes and Judy Carl-Hendrick of Intercultural Press for their usual thoughtful editing, and to Patty Topel whose designs bring my prose to life.

My pal Toby Frank gets the last word (nothing unusual in that). She has a way of working with writers that makes you feel like yours is the only book that really matters. We writers all know that, of course, but it's rare to find a publisher who does.

—Craig Storti
Westminster, Maryland
Fall 1998

Introduction

This book is for anyone who needs to understand people from a different culture. Whether you're a foreigner—living, working, or going to school in another country—or you're at home, living and working with people *from* other countries, this volume will take you into the minds of people from abroad and help you understand why they think and act the way they do. No matter what culture you come from or what culture or cultures you need to learn about, you will find important and useful information in these pages. Moreover, if you live in a country with distinct regional, ethnic, or racial differences, you will find help here in crossing those boundaries too.

Few of us live any longer in a monocultural world. We work with people from other cultures, live next door to them, study in class with them, or teach them. They may be our customers, our competition, or our in-laws. Even those of us who do inhabit the odd patch of cultural homogeneity surely sense the wider multicultural world pressing ever harder on our borders. To know only your own culture is increasingly an artifact of an earlier, preglobal age.

But it is more than an artifact, of course; depending on the circumstances, ignorance of other cultures can also be a disadvantage and a distinct liability. It can cost you money, friends, business, and professional advancement. At best, it is personally limiting; at worst, it alienates and hurts those around you. Cross-cultural awareness and sensitivity are no longer just the subjects of college courses or seminars for globe-trotting executives; they are basic survival skills for almost everyone.

What I say is this [the Indian man remarked] and this I do not say to all Englishmen: God made us different, you and I, and your fathers and my fathers. For one thing, we have not the same notions of honesty and speaking the truth. That is not our fault, because we are made so. And look now what you do? You come and judge us by your own standards of morality. You are, of course, too hard on us. And again I tell you you are great fools in this matter. Who are we to have your morals, or you to have ours?

—Rudyard Kipling
"East and West"

But I'm Good with People

This is fine, you say, but I deal with people who are different from me all the time. What's so special about people from other cultures that I suddenly need all this help?

It's a fair question, for when you come right down to it, no two people, whoever they are, are exactly alike. But what's special about people from other cultures is not simply that they are different from you, but the *degree* to which they are different. After all, people from your own culture, as unlike you as they may be, still hold many of the same fundamental values and beliefs that you do. Chances are that what you think of as right and good, they also think of as right and good. And what is natural and normal to them is also natural and normal to you. You and they grew up with a similar worldview and understanding of reality. What differences there are between you are more likely to be the result of personality and family background than of basic values and beliefs.

With people from other cultures, however, while there may very well be differences of personality and background, there are likely to be more profound differences in values, beliefs, and worldviews. This is a scale of difference that puts cross-cultural encounters in a separate category from same-culture experiences of difference.

This is not to say, however, that every encounter between people from two distinct cultures is automatically going to be more confusing and difficult than encounters between people from the same culture, only that the *potential* for misunderstanding is almost always greater. Nor does this mean that the skills you already use in dealing with other people no longer apply when you interact with a foreigner.*

But it does mean that whatever skills you now bring to bear in dealing with people different from you, regardless of the nature or extent of that difference, are going to be needed all the more and in settings and circumstances where you may never have had to apply them before. Moreover, your skills notwith-

---

* Each of us, of course, is a foreigner everywhere but in our home culture. As Ogden Nash has written, "Where you're at / is your habitat. Everywhere else / you're a foreigner."

standing, you are almost certainly going to need information and knowledge (about other cultures) that you may not now possess.

Why a Workbook?

You could, of course, read a book about cultural differences—there are many excellent titles—and benefit greatly as a result. But a workbook such as this offers you something more: the chance to encounter and confront culture, to interact with and respond to it. In the process, culture will become something real and alive, something you have to deal with, not merely think about. The hope is that whatever you learn about culture through such a direct encounter will make a greater impact on you and stay with you longer.

Generalizations

We will be obliged to use a number of generalizations in this workbook. It's not possible to talk about culture, about groups of people, without making generalizations. Yet we all know that generalizations, however true they may be of groups, are not always fair to or accurate about individuals within a group. Or, for that matter, are they necessarily always true even of groups. This gives generalizations a bad name and makes people understandably wary of them.

This book can't sidestep that dilemma any more than any other book on this subject can, but we can at least issue a warning: always remember that cultural generalizations are necessarily statements of likelihood and potential, not of certainty. By definition, a generalization is taken out of context; to generalize, after all, means to deliberately ignore the particular and the specific. Hence, a generalization can tell you at best how people from a particular culture *may* behave in a given situation but not necessarily how they *will* behave nor how they will *always* behave.

In the end, what a particular individual does in a particular situation will depend in part on culture and in part on the circumstances. Or, to put this another way, a person's culture is *one* of the circumstances that will influence his or her behavior in a given situation. In any cross-cultural interaction, then, feel free to bring along with you whatever you may know about the other person's culture, but be ready to set such generalizations aside when they are clearly not meaningful. Perhaps the best advice about generalizations is never to automatically rule them in—or out—in any situation.

With this warning firmly in mind, you should not hesitate to embrace cultural generalizations, examining and mining them for the kernel of truth they often contain. Nor should you hesitate to make cross-cultural comparisons, putting a generalization about one culture up against a generalization about another. If you treat them with respect, generalizations will repay your consideration.

The Whole and the Parts

Culture is a complex concept, a whole made up of numerous interlocking parts, each interacting with others to create various effects. In this book, the parts of culture have been separated out and presented in isolation. While this approach makes culture more accessible and easier to examine, it also risks reducing culture to a series of abstractions. And the problem with culture as abstraction is that it suggests that culture could somehow exist independent of people, that culture could take on meaning or significance apart from the behavior of the people who embody culture and make it real. While it can indeed be described and understood in the abstract, reduced, in effect, to concept and theory, you must remember that you will never encounter it in such a bloodless form. The essence of culture is behavior, and only people, not concepts, can behave.

With these few remarks and caveats to guide you, you're invited to turn the page and plunge into the world of cross-cultural interaction. Be advised that while there is a certain logic to the sequence of chapters and exercises, with later exercises building on earlier ones, you should feel free to dip into this workbook at will and do the exercises in any order you choose. It's a good idea, however, to complete chapter 1—it's only three exercises—before you get too far into the rest of the workbook.

What Is Culture?

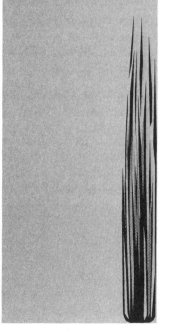

To realize it takes all sorts to make a world, one must have seen a certain number of the sorts with one's own eyes. There is all the difference in the world between believing academically, with the intellect, and believing personally, with the whole living self.
—Aldous Huxley
Jesting Pilate

For the most part this book will focus on cultural differences, on the ways in which a person from one culture thinks and behaves differently from a person from another. It is these differences, after all, which cause most of the confusion, frustration, sometimes even hostility that occur when people from different cultures interact with each other. Before you can fully understand and appreciate cultural differences, however, you first need to understand what culture itself is and how it operates, which is the purpose of this brief opening chapter.

The best place to start is with a definition of culture. Two researchers in the 1960s are reported to have found over three hundred definitions of culture, and there are no doubt many more in existence today. Fortunately, most of these definitions contain many of the same elements, which suggests that there is a common core to what observers in the field think of as culture. For the purposes of this workbook, the following definition will suffice:

> Culture is the shared assumptions, values, and beliefs of a group of people which result in characteristic behaviors.

This definition captures two essential points about culture: that it has an invisible dimension (assumptions, values, and beliefs) and a visible dimension (behavior) and that these two dimensions relate to each other as cause and effect, respectively. Practically speaking, what this means is that behavior—the things people do and say—is neither arbitrary nor spontaneous. That is, people don't make up their behavior as they go along; they don't wake up saying, "I think I'll act like this today." Rather, behavior is a direct result of what people assume, value, or believe in. Indeed, when we say that someone's behavior "makes no sense," what we really mean is that that person's behavior is not consistent with what we know he or she believes in or holds dear.

Understanding the cause-and-effect relationship between the two dimensions of culture is essential to any kind of successful cross-cultural undertaking, for once you grasp that behavior is tied to values and beliefs, then it's not difficult to accept that people with different values and beliefs—such as a person from another culture—are going to *behave* differently from you. Nor should it be difficult to then go one step further and accept that that other person's behavior, no matter how different from your own, probably makes perfect sense to that individual and other members of his or her culture.

With this definition of culture to guide you, move on now to the three exercises in this chapter. They will explore the concept of culture in more detail and provide you with a firm foundation for examining the cultural differences that are the focus of the rest of this workbook.

Matching Values and Behavior

This exercise demonstrates one of the key features of culture just described: the cause-and-effect relationship between people's assumptions, values, and beliefs (the invisible side of culture) and their behavior (the visible side). This relationship is at the heart of culture, which is to say that there can be no real understanding of culture if this relationship is not likewise understood.

Below you will find a list of ten values or beliefs on the left side and ten behaviors on the right. Match each value or belief with a behavior which someone who holds that value is likely to exhibit.

The portion we see of human beings is very small: their forms and faces, voices and words.... [But] beyond these, like an immense dark continent, lies all that has made them.

—Freya Stark
The Journey's Echo

1. Being direct
2. Centrality of family
3. Fatalism
4. Saving face
5. Respect for age
6. Informality
7. Deference to authority
8. Being indirect

_____ Use of understatement

_____ Asking people to call you by your first name

_____ Taking off from work to attend the funeral of a cousin

_____ Not asking for help from the person next to you on an exam

_____ Disagreeing openly with someone at a meeting

_____ Not laying off an older worker whose performance is weak

_____ At a meeting, agreeing with a suggestion you think is wrong

_____ Inviting the teaboy to eat lunch with you in your office

9. Self-reliance   _____ Asking the boss's opinion of something you're the expert on

10. Egalitarianism   _____ Accepting, without question, that something cannot be changed

Suggested Answers

_8_ Use of understatement

_6_ Asking people to call you by your first name

_2_ Taking off from work to attend the funeral of a cousin

_9_ Not asking for help from the person next to you on an exam

_1_ Disagreeing openly with someone at a meeting

_5_ Not laying off an older worker whose performance is weak

_4_ At a meeting, agreeing with a suggestion you think is wrong

_10_ Inviting the teaboy to eat lunch with you in your office

_7_ Asking the boss's opinion of something you're the expert on

_3_ Accepting, without question, that something cannot be changed

"How" Does a Behavior Mean?

I grew up in Iowa and I knew what to do with butter: you put it on roasting ears [of corn], pancakes, and popcorn. Then I went to France and saw a Frenchman put butter on radishes. I waited for the Cosmic Revenge—for the Eiffel Tower to topple, the Seine to sizzle, or the grape to wither on the vine. But...the universe continued unperturbed.

—Genelle Morain
Toward Internationalism

People are in the habit of thinking that behavior has inherent meaning, something attached to the behavior that enables people to understand it, that somehow makes it mean this and not that. In fact, for all practical purposes, an instance of behavior has no particular meaning other than what the people who witness that behavior assign to it. In short, behavior means what we *decide* it means—and very often it means nothing at all.

The truth of this is easy enough to demonstrate. Take a simple gesture, such as the American okay sign: the thumb and forefinger meet to make a circle and the remaining three fingers are held aloft. In the United States this behavior means okay or all right (and also designates zero). In parts of the Mediterranean and Latin America, it is an obscene gesture. In Japan it designates coins (as opposed to paper money). And there are no doubt many places where it has other meanings or even no meaning at all. This gesture or piece of behavior does not somehow carry its meaning within it; meaning is imposed on it (or not) by those who observe it.

When the people attaching meaning to a behavior are from the same culture, they are likely to attach the same meaning, resulting in successful communication. But when they are from different cultures, they may take the same behavior to mean very different things. This phenomenon, different people assigning different meanings to the same behavior, is at the heart of most cross-cultural misunderstandings. The exercise which follows illustrates how this can happen.

Part 1

Read the description of the eight instances of behavior given below and write down your immediate response to or interpretation of that behavior (what meaning *you* would assign to the behavior). The first one has been done for you.

1. A person comes to a meeting half an hour after the stated starting time.
   Your interpretation: *This person is late and should at least apologize or give an explanation.*

2. Someone kicks a dog.
   Your interpretation: _____

   _____

3. At the end of a meal, people belch audibly.
   Your interpretation: _____

   _____

4. The young person you are talking to does not look you in the eye.
   Your interpretation: _____

   _____

5. A woman carries a heavy pile of wood on her back, while her husband walks in front of her carrying nothing.
   Your interpretation: _____

   _____

6. A male guest helps a hostess carry dirty dishes into the kitchen.
   Your interpretation: _____

   _____

7. A young man and a young woman are kissing on a park bench.
   Your interpretation: _____

   _____

8. While taking an exam, a student copies from the paper of another student.
   Your interpretation: _____

   _____

Part 2

In the second part of this activity, you will find the same eight behaviors from Part 1, but you are now being asked to imagine the meaning these behaviors would have in a culture different from your own. The particular cultural difference is described in each case. Read each behavior and the description of the culture and then write in the space provided what meaning you think a person from that culture would assign to the behavior.

1. A person comes to a meeting half an hour after the stated starting time. How would this act be interpreted by
   - someone from a culture where people always arrive half an hour after the stated starting time?
   Interpretation: _____

   _____

   - someone from a culture where meetings never start until at least an hour after the stated time?
   Interpretation: _____

   _____

2. Someone kicks a dog. How would this act be interpreted by
   - someone from a country where dogs always carry disease?
   Interpretation: _____

   _____

   - someone from a country where dogs are not kept as pets and are usually vicious?
   Interpretation: _____

   _____

3. At the end of a meal, people belch audibly. How would this be interpreted by
   - someone from a culture where belching is the normal way to compliment the food?
   Interpretation: _____

   _____

4. The young person you are talking to does not look you in the eye. How would this be interpreted by
   - someone in whose culture it is considered rude to make eye contact when listening to older or senior people?
   Interpretation: _____

   _____

5. A woman carries a heavy pile of wood on her back, while her husband walks in front of her carrying nothing. How would this be interpreted by
   - someone from a culture where men never carry wood?
   Interpretation: _____

   _____

6. A male guest helps a hostess carry dirty dishes into the kitchen. How would this act be interpreted by
   - men from a culture where men never clean up after a meal?
   Interpretation: _____

   _____

   - the hostess from that same culture?
   Interpretation: _____

   _____

7. A young man and a young woman are kissing on a park bench. How would this act be interpreted by
   - someone from a culture where men and women never touch in public?
   Interpretation: _____

   _____

8. While taking an exam, a student copies from the paper of another student. How would this act be interpreted by
   - someone from a culture where exams are not fair and are designed to eliminate students at various stages of the education system?
   Interpretation: _____

   _____

- someone from a culture where it is shameful not to help your friend if you are able to?
  Interpretation: _____

_____

What have you learned from this exercise? Probably that you shouldn't be too quick to judge other people's behavior, at least not from your own point of view. The wiser course in any cross-cultural situation is to suspend interpretation or judgment, suspend the assigning of meaning until you can find out what any given behavior might signify in the other person's culture. Then you will at least be able to interpret the behavior "correctly."

This does not mean, by the way, that you will necessarily like or approve of the behavior at that point; it merely means that you will probably understand what lies behind it, the logic of the behavior in that culture. In some cases, knowing why people behave in a certain way—for example, learning that people keep dogs away for fear of disease—may cause you to change your opinion of the behavior and the person. In other cases, however, knowing why people behave as they do will not change your opinion. The point is not that you should always be able to like or accept the different behaviors of people from other cultures, but only that you should reserve judgment until you have understood them. Indeed, that rule applies to any kind of interaction, whether cross-cultural or not. But once you *have* understood, then you are in a better position to judge.

Finally, you will note that this exercise has deliberately selected behaviors that exist in two or more cultures but have different meanings—the usual suspects in cross-cultural misunderstandings. There are, however, many cross-cultural situations where the confusion is not caused by different interpretations of a shared behavior but by the fact that what is a behavior in one culture, such as a gesture, is in fact not behavior—because it has no meaning—in another culture. This common scenario will be examined in chapter 3.

What Culture Is Not

Not all behavior is cultural. There are many behaviors, many things people do and say, that are neither caused by nor related to their culture. If all human behavior were put on a continuum, that part related to culture would fall in the middle, between universal at one extreme and personal at the other. The point of this exercise is, precisely, to put culture in its place.

Universal behaviors are those which apply to everyone, regardless of culture, what is usually referred to as "human nature." All people in all cultures eat regularly; eating is not French or Indonesian or Kenyan. The French prepare and eat different foods than do Kenyans, with different social customs involved, but the act of eating is universal—as are using language, seeking shelter, and raising children. In a book like this, which focuses on culture and cultural differences, it's easy to give culture more credit than it is due, to get the impression that *everything* about a person from Culture A is going to be different from *everything* about a person from Culture B, and to conclude therefore that all cross-cultural interactions by definition are going to be difficult. But this would be to overlook those many universal assumptions, values, and behaviors which transcend culture, those numerous ways in which all people are alike. In short, while cultural factors will play a part in most cross-cultural interactions, causing the usual complications, universal factors will also be present, making things somewhat easier.

At the opposite end of the behavioral continuum from the universal lies the personal. While shared assumptions, values, and beliefs guarantee that people from the same culture will be similar in many ways, personal experience guarantees that no two people from the same culture will be identical. To put it another way, each of us is in part a product of culture (and to that extent similar to others from the same culture) and in part

It began to dawn on them that beyond the teeming romance that lies in the differences between men—the diversity of their homes, the multitude of their ways, the dividing strangeness of their faces and tongues—there lies the still profounder romance of their kinship with each other, the immutable constancy of man's need to share laughter and friendship, poetry and love in common.

—Arthur Grimble
A Pattern of Islands

a product of our own unique life circumstances (and to that extent like no one else anywhere).

The news here for the culture crosser is not nearly as good, for while the phenomenon of universal behavior makes cross-cultural interaction potentially easier, the phenomenon of personal behavior makes all interactions potentially more complicated. It means that the behavior you might predict or expect of someone, based on what you have learned about his or her culture, will not necessarily occur in any given interaction because a personal influence might override a cultural inclination. In other words, in the right circumstances cultural information will be very useful to you in dealing with foreigners, but it will not always be an accurate predictor of how someone is going to behave.

To recap, then, each of us is like everybody else in some ways (universal behaviors), like the people in our culture in some other ways (cultural behaviors), and like no one else at all in still other ways (personal behaviors). The following exercise will help make this point clear. For each of the sixteen items, put a *U*, *C*, or *P* in the blank depending on whether you think the behavior is Universal, Cultural, or Personal. (Note that something that is personal could, of course, be done by a number of people in the same culture, but it would only be cultural if it were done by most of the people from that culture.) A few items might be either cultural or personal.

____	1.	Sleeping with a bedroom window open
____	2.	Running from a dangerous animal
____	3.	Considering snakes to be "evil"
____	4.	Men opening doors for women
____	5.	Respecting older people
____	6.	Learning one's native language
____	7.	Speaking Arabic
____	8.	Speaking Arabic as a foreign language
____	9.	Eating regularly
____	10.	Eating with a knife, fork, and spoon
____	11.	Liking the novels of Charles Dickens

___ 12. Calling a waiter with a hissing sound

___ 13. Regretting being the cause of an accident

___ 14. Feeling sad at the death of your mother

___ 15. Wearing white mourning robes for thirty days after the death of your mother

___ 16. Disliking having to wear mourning clothes for thirty days after the death of your mother

Suggested Answers

_P_ 1. Sleeping with a bedroom window open

_U_ 2. Running from a dangerous animal. [Note that what is considered a dangerous animal might differ from culture to culture.]

_C_ 3. Considering snakes to be "evil"

_C_ 4. Men opening doors for women

_C_ 5. Respecting older people

_U_ 6. Learning one's native language

_C_ 7. Speaking Arabic

_P_ 8. Speaking Arabic as a foreign language

_U_ 9. Eating regularly

_C_ 10. Eating with a knife, fork, and spoon

_P_ 11. Liking the novels of Charles Dickens

_C_ 12. Calling a waiter with a hissing sound

_U_ 13. Regretting being the cause of an accident

_U_ 14. Feeling sad at the death of your mother

_C_ 15. Wearing white mourning robes for thirty days after the death of your mother

_P_ 16. Disliking having to wear mourning clothes for thirty days after the death of your mother

Building Blocks of Culture

This section of the workbook introduces you to four fundamental dimensions or building blocks of culture which correspond to four broad categories of the human experience. The values and beliefs associated with these four dimensions are the source of and explanation for a wide variety of behavior. To understand these four concepts, then, and in particular the different ways they manifest themselves in different cultures, is to take a giant step along the road to cultural awareness and sensitivity.

These four building blocks are

- Concept of self—individualist and collectivist
- Personal versus societal responsibility—universalist and particularist
- Concept of time—monochronic and polychronic
- Locus of control—internal and external

Because these topics are so fundamental to an understanding of cultural differences, underscoring and influencing a wide variety of human activity, they will be examined in some detail in this chapter, each building block being the subject of five separate exercises:

1. a brief introductory exercise
2. a defining exercise
3. a self-scoring exercise
4. an application exercise
5. a cultural comparison exercise

When you have finished with each building block, you will have a deeper appreciation of the scope of these dimensions of the human experience, of the different forms they take in different cultures, and of what you can do when confronted with them.

Truth is not that which can be demonstrated by the aid of logic. If orange trees are hardy and rich in fruit in this bit of soil and not in that, then this bit of soil is what is truth for orange trees. If a particular religion or culture or scale of values, if one form of activity rather than another, brings self-fulfillment to a man, releases the prince asleep within him...then that scale of values, that culure, that form of activity constitute his truth. Logic you say? Let logic wangle its own explanation of life.

—Antoine de
Saint-Exupéry
Wind, Sand and Stars

Exercise 2.1

Dialogues

What strikes me the most upon the whole is the total difference of manners between them and us, from the greatest object to the least. There is not the smallest similitude in the twenty-four hours.

—Horace Walpole
Letters

Each of the next three chapters in this book will begin with what is called a diagnostic exercise, a kind of pretest which will expose you to the major concepts of the chapter and measure your knowledge of those concepts before you actually begin studying them. Then, when you have finished the chapter, you can take the test again and, so the thinking goes, do much better on it, thereby demonstrating how much you have learned.

In each case, the diagnostic exercise will be called *dialogues*.[1] For the purposes of this workbook, a "dialogue" is defined as "a short conversation between speakers from two different cultures which illustrates a particular cultural difference." Your task is to read each dialogue and try to identify what that difference is. Be advised that a dialogue is deliberately written in such a way that the cultural difference will not be obvious—just as it is not obvious to speakers in similar real-life conversations. If you can't see it, don't worry; the information in the rest of the chapter will help you get to the bottom of the dialogues.

You may feel, incidentally, that the speakers in these dialogues need not come from different cultures in order to have these conversations, that the misunderstanding or confusion could easily occur between two speakers from the same culture. That is entirely possible, of course; the point here is not that a cultural difference is the *only* explanation for these kinds of misunderstandings, but that when the two parties involved come from different cultures, it is always a possible explanation.

After you have tried to figure out the dialogues, you should go ahead and complete the other exercises in this chapter. Later,

---

[1] The dialogue concept, the notion of burying a cultural difference inside an innocuous conversational exchange, was first developed by Alfred Kraemer, to whom the present writer is greatly indebted.

when you finish the chapter, you will be asked to return to these dialogues and analyze them again in light of what you will then know about the building blocks of culture. With any luck, the cultural difference buried in each dialogue will suddenly jump out at you.

You will, incidentally, find the "answers" to these dialogues—an explanation of what was happening in each one—at the end of this chapter in the section called "Dialogues Revisited" (pages 83-85). While you might be tempted to read these answers now, before working the intervening exercises, you are strongly encouraged to hold off. If you curb your curiosity now and then reread the dialogues as recommended, you will have the distinct pleasure of figuring them out on your own!

1. Near the Family

SHARON: So, Fatima, you'll be graduating in May. Congratulations.

FATIMA: Thank you.

SHARON: Do you have a job lined up?

FATIMA: Yes. I'll be working for the Central Bank.

SHARON: Good for you. Have you found a place to live yet?

FATIMA: Actually, the bank's very near my parents' place.

SHARON: That's nice. So you'll be living quite near them.

2. Vacancy

HORST: Have you finished writing that job advertisement yet?

LUIGI: Not quite.

HORST: Don't take too long. Filling that vacancy is a priority.

LUIGI: I agree. Actually, I think I know of a possible candidate.

HORST: You do? Who?

LUIGI: She's my youngest niece, Marta. A nice girl.

HORST: Great! Tell her to apply.

3. Helping Miss Thomas

ROBERTO: Miss Thomas! How nice to see you.

MISS THOMAS: How are you, Roberto?

ROBERTO: Fine, fine. Thank you. What can I get for you?

MISS THOMAS: Well, to start with I'd like half a dozen eggs.

ROBERTO: Yes.

MISS THOMAS: And then I'd like some butter.

ROBERTO: Yes. Ah, Octavio! Good to see you. How are you?

OCTAVIO: Fine, thanks. And you?

ROBERTO: Fine. How can I help you?

OCTAVIO: I need some bananas.

ROBERTO: Of course. Rosita! How are you? I haven't seen you in a long time. How is that little boy of yours?

ROSITA: He's very well.

ROBERTO: What can I do for you?

MISS THOMAS: Roberto! I thought you were helping me.

ROBERTO: But I am helping you, Miss Thomas.

4. Out of Order

MIRANDA: Excuse me, but the elevator is out of order.

LARISA: Really? Whom should we talk to?

MIRANDA: Talk to?

LARISA: To report it.

MIRANDA: I have no idea.

LARISA: Oh, I'm sorry. I thought you lived here too.

MIRANDA: But I do.

Exercise 2.2

Dividing the Spoils

This exercise is a brief introduction to the first of the four building blocks, the concept of the self. The two poles of this dimension, individualism and collectivism, will be defined in the exercise immediately following this one.

For six weeks, you and the three other people in your division have been working on an important special project. Now the work is done and the four of you have been awarded a cash prize of $20,000. How should this money be distributed? In answering this question, you may find the following information useful:

1. Person A did 25 percent of the work.
2. Person B did 40 percent of the work.
3. Person C did 25 percent of the work.
4. Person D did 10 percent of the work.

Write in the amount of the cash prize you think each member of the team should get:

Person A: $ _____

Person B: $ _____

Person C: $ _____

Person D: $ _____

Now read the discussion on the following page to see how respondents from individualist and collectivist cultures typically differ in their answers to this question.

The Japanese regard individuality as evidence of immaturity, and autonomy as the freedom to comply with one's obligations and duties.

—W. M. Fox
"Japanese Management:
Tradition under Strain"
Business Horizons

Discussion

Typical answer from members of individualist cultures:

Person A: $5,000 (or 25%)
Person B: $8,000 (40%)
Person C: $5,000 (25%)
Person D: $2,000 (10%)

Typical answer from members of collectivist cultures:

Person A: $5,000
Person B: $5,000
Person C: $5,000
Person D: $5,000

People from more collectivist cultures believe that their own security and well-being ultimately depend on the well-being and survival of their group. A group is only as strong as its weakest members, of course, so dividing the spoils evenly—increasing the well-being of everyone in the group equally—offers the greatest protection for all members.

People from more individualist cultures believe rewards should be directly commensurate with one's level of effort.

Individualist-Collectivist

People in different cultures have different notions of personal identity, spanning a wide range of alternatives, from *collectivism* at one extreme to *individualism* at the other.[1] The two poles of this building block are defined below:

> *Individualist*: The smallest unit of survival is the individual. People identify primarily with self, and the needs of the individual are satisfied before those of the group. Looking after and taking care of oneself, being self-sufficient, guarantees the well-being of the group. Independence and self-reliance are stressed and greatly valued, and personal freedom is highly desired. In general, there is more psychological and emotional distance from others. One may choose to join groups, but group membership is not essential to one's identity, survival, or success.

> *Collectivist*[2]: The primary group, usually the immediate family, is the smallest unit of survival. One's identity is in large part a function of one's membership and role in a group (e.g., the family, the work team). The survival and success of the group ensures the well-being of the individual, so that by considering

I had noticed in several prior conversations with Bolivar his difficulty distinguishing between his own likes and dislikes on the one hand and what he saw as best for the community as a whole on the other. It came through in his way of using "we" over "I" much of the time.

—Mike Tidwell
Amazon Stranger

---

[1] The exercises in this building block derive in part from the excellent work of Harry Triandis and Geert Hofstede on the individualism/collectivism dichotomy. See Hofstede entry in Recommended Reading.

[2] *Collectivism* and *collectivist* are highly charged words in many countries, with strong political overtones. These words are used here in their strict ethnological sense, as opposites of *individualism* and *individualist*, and should not be construed as referring to any political ideology. Alternatives might have been found, but the individualist-collectivist formulation is so widely used in the intercultural field that it would have been a disservice to readers to have invented an artificial substitute.

the needs and feelings of others, one protects one-self. Harmony and the interdependence of group members are stressed and valued. There is relatively little psychological or emotional distance between group members, though there is more distance between group and nongroup members (ingroups and out-groups).

No culture, of course, will be exclusively individualist or collectivist—all cultures will have elements of both poles—but cultures do tend to be *more* one than the other. Because of personal differences (see exercise 1.3), individuals in a given culture could of course be anywhere along the continuum—though they are more likely to be on the same side as their culture—and may very well be at one spot in one set of circumstances and somewhere else in another. Personal differences notwithstanding, it is important to understand these two poles and the numerous cultural behaviors they account for.

The exercise which follows asks you to take the definitions of *individualism* and *collectivism* presented above and apply them to specific examples of behavior. Below you will find a list of twelve items, each of which is more representative of one pole of this dimension than the other. Read each item and put an *I* next to those behaviors more consistent with individualism and a *C* next to those more consistent with collectivism.

_____ 1. Companies give employee-of-the-year awards.

_____ 2. Harmony and saving face are highly valued.

_____ 3. Friendships tend to be somewhat opportunistic; people have many friends.

_____ 4. Promotion is based on output, measurable results.

_____ 5. There is less of a need for signed contracts in business.

_____ 6. Friendships are for life; people have one or two close friends.

_____ 7. It's okay to stand out.

_____ 8. A mother asks her four-year-old what he or she wants to wear today.

_____ 9. Self-help books are popular.

_____ 10. Consensus decision making is the norm.

_____ 11. The language has one word for "mother's brother," another for "father's brother."

_____ 12. Arranged marriages are common.

Suggested Answers

_I_ 1. Singling out people for individual recognition is, of course, individualistic.

_C_ 2. This is the glue that binds collectivists together.

_I_ 3. In collectivist cultures friendships are automatic, as a result of ingroup membership.

_I_ 4. Individualists tend to define themselves more in terms of what they accomplish than by their personal qualities.

_C_ 5. People do business with members of their group or with people known to members of their group—in other words, with people they know they can trust.

_C_ 6. The bonds of collectivists are strong and enduring.

_I_ 7. Collectivists are generally more comfortable with group rather than personal recognition.

_I_ 8. Fostering self-reliance and independence is individualistic.

_I_ 9. This is self-reliance again.

_C_ 10. Trying to get all members to agree and thereby preserving harmony is classic collectivist behavior.

_C_ 11. In close-knit primary groups, people tend to play distinct roles, and names are needed to distinguish the players from each other.

_C_ 12. The primary group, the family, must play a major role when new members, such as a proposed spouse, join the group.

Choices

This exercise introduces additional aspects of the individualist/collectivist building block and reviews some of those from exercise 2.3. It also asks you to think about your own self-concept in this context. Below you will find ten sets of paired statements, *a* and *b*. Read each pair and circle the number of the one which best describes the way you feel or the action you would take vis-à-vis that item. Please choose one even if you think that both alternatives are true or possible. For many of the examples, you might also be tempted to say, "It depends on the situation," which indeed it does. But choose anyway, without thinking too much!

When someone says privacy, I think of loneliness.
—Ethiopian student in
John Fieg and John Blair
There Is a Difference

_____ 1a. Managers should be hired from within the organization, based mainly on their seniority.

_____ 1b. Managers should be hired on the basis of their skills and previous experience in similar jobs.

_____ 2a. It takes a long time to make a new friend.

_____ 2b. Friends can be made relatively quickly.

_____ 3a. If I took a job with a new company, I would expect my old employer to wish me well.

_____ 3b. If I took a job with a new company, I would be afraid that my present employer might lose face.

_____ 4a. I expect people to judge me by my achievements.

_____ 4b. I expect people to judge me by the groups I belong to.

_____ 5a. Before making a decision, it is best to make sure everyone agrees with it.

_____ 5b. Before making a decision, you should get at least half of the people to agree with it.

_____ 6a. I am embarrassed by individual recognition.

_____ 6b. If I do a good job, I feel I have earned individual recognition.

_____ 7a. Making sure people don't lose face is more important than always being completely honest.

_____ 7b. Being honest with people is always best in the end.

_____ 8a. If my brother did wrong, I would admit it to other people.

_____ 8b. If my brother did wrong, I would defend him to other people.

_____ 9a. Confrontation is sometimes necessary to clear the air.

_____ 9b. Confrontation almost always causes more problems than it solves.

_____ 10a. In the end, you can always rely on other people.

_____ 10b. In the end, you can only rely on yourself.

Now that you have circled your choices, read all the items again and decide which are more consistent with individualism (put an *I* in the blank) and which with collectivism (put a *C*). Then check your answers. How many of your circled choices turned out to be individualist and how many collectivist?

This exercise isn't scientific, of course, and doesn't "prove" anything about you. For one thing, all the items, as noted earlier, are taken out of context; you might very well select one alternative in one set of circumstances and the other in another set. Moreover, the choices you made for any given item may have more to do with some other aspect of your personality than your individualist or collectivist tendencies. Even so, you have no doubt been given some food for thought and also been exposed to additional contexts in which this important concept operates and additional circumstances under which it might influence people's behavior.

Suggested Answers

Remember that an item marked *I* or *C* means only that the particular behavior tends to be *more* characteristic of an Individualist or a Collectivist but is by no means exclusive to members of that category.

1a. *C*

1b. *I*

2a. *C*

2b. *I*

3a. *I*

3b. *C*

4a. *I*

4b. *C*

5a. *C*

5b. *I*

6a. *C*

6b. *I*

7a. *C*

7b. *I*

8a. *I*

8b. *C*

9a. *I*

9b. *C*

10a. *C*

10b. *I*

Exercise 2.5

What Would You Do?

[W]hen a psychiatric clinic was first set up in a rural district of Nigeria..., the family invariably accompanied the sufferer and insisted on being present at the patient's interview with the psychiatrist. The idea that the patient might exist as an individual apart from the family...did not occur to Nigerians who were still living a traditional village life.

—Anthony Storr
Solitude: A Return to the Self

Now that you have spent a good bit of time in the company of the individualist/collectivist dichotomy, the moment has come to begin applying what you have learned. In this exercise, you will be presented with two situations where differences involving this aspect of culture have caused an incident. These may be situations you have been in or can imagine being in. In any case, a successful resolution of each incident requires putting into practice what you know about this concept of self. Read each incident and jot down in the space below it what you would do or say if you were faced with the situation.

1. Teamwork

You come from a culture where people prefer to work in teams and where the success of the team guarantees the well-being of the individual members. You believe that a group of people is more likely to meet with success if they work as a team than if they work independently. But in the culture where you now live and work, most of your colleagues prefer to work on their own, to succeed or fail based on their own individual actions, and they expect you to depend on yourself as well. While they help each other as necessary, it is not considered professional to need too much help.

In dealing with them, you have tried to work collaboratively, offering assistance wherever you saw it was needed—assistance that was often very much appreciated—and expecting assistance in return. You have noticed, however, that whenever you have asked for help, your colleagues have been somewhat surprised and reluctant. One day you confronted one of your colleagues on this issue. You pointed out that you helped her a few days ago when she was behind on a project, but this week when you asked for her help, she said she was too busy. You asked her why she thought it was okay to take help but not to give it in return. She looked surprised and said, "But I never asked for your help. I thought you were just being kind. I certainly don't expect that kind of help." What should you do in this situation?

_____

_____

_____

2. Telling It Like It Is

You are working in a culture where people tend to be more collectivist, especially in the sense that group harmony and saving face are highly valued. You, on the other hand, feel that while harmony and saving face are good things in general, they can sometimes be more trouble than they're worth. You've noticed, for example, that people tend to tell you what they think you want to hear rather than the truth, especially if the truth isn't particularly pleasant. This bothers you because you take people at their word; you assume they mean what they say, or they wouldn't say it. You're not sure anymore if you can trust what people are telling you, if you can act on what they say.

At the same time, you're beginning to sense that you may be rubbing some people the wrong way by "telling it like it is." Today, any doubts you had about this were removed when your manager called you into his office. He said several colleagues had complained that you weren't "very careful" in how you spoke, that you said things "more strongly" than was necessary, and that you didn't take people's feelings into account. What would you do if you were in this situation?

_____

_____

_____

Discussion

Each of these incidents raises the same basic issue: What does a person on one side of the individualist/collectivist divide do when working in a culture that is on the other side? What adjustments in his or her behavior and attitudes might be expected and appreciated by members of the other culture? People in these situations do not *have* to make these adjustments, of course, but they should at least understand the consequences of not doing so.

1. Teamwork

This incident explores the question of what a person who is more of a collectivist must do to work effectively in a culture that is more individualistic. To begin with, you should not be offended by the woman who readily accepted your help but was surprised to be asked to reciprocate. From her point of view, when you offered to help her, it was sheer generosity on your part and not because you felt any particular obligation; she probably even wondered how it was you had so much free time that you were able to offer help. And she certainly did not feel, when she accepted your help, that she was thereby incurring any kind of obligation to help you in similar circumstances. She is, therefore, genuinely surprised when you seem upset because she didn't help you when you asked.

As a collectivist, you will have to learn to work more on your own in an individualist environment, which may mean, by the way, that you won't have much time to help others with their work. You may find this difficult and against your instincts, but you must keep in mind that your superiors and colleagues are going to expect you to get all your work done, and it will not matter to them that the reason you're behind is that you've been helping other people. As for those other people, you must realize that they may very well accept your help if you offer it, but they certainly do not expect it, nor do they feel that this means they have to help you in return. They will assume, rather, that you are very kind and seem to have a lot of spare time!

Finally, this does not mean that people in individualist cultures never work in teams or help each other out, but it does mean that they may do this less often than you are used to.

2. Telling It Like It Is

This incident highlights the trouble an individualist can get into in a more collectivist society, where people are careful what they say to one another in order to preserve harmony and face. As an individualist in such a setting, you have two tasks: (1) to learn how to read between the lines in what people say and (2) to learn how to phrase what you say more indirectly (so that others will get the message by reading between the lines).

You are used to taking people at their word, which means you assume people say what they mean. But in cultures where people don't, you will have to get into the habit of thinking what *else* people's words could mean in addition to the literal meaning. You will also need to pay more attention to the nonverbal cues accompanying people's words (which are, incidentally, culture-specific), for these often convey more of the message than the spoken word. Finally, you will need to pay more attention to what people do not say, for this can also be a large part of the message.

As for your own speech, as your manager has just told you, you will have to get into the habit of being more indirect, saying less and implying more, saying half of what you mean, perhaps, rather than the whole of it. You may also want to use third parties to deliver messages, what you would probably call "going behind someone's back," and they might call "using a go-between," for this allows people to save face more easily. And you can always try to express more of your message through nonverbal channels and through the things you elect not to say.

Exercise 2.6

An Accident

Abstract consequences, like right and wrong or truth and untruth, depend on the circumstances. Behavior that is acceptable in one situation may be unacceptable in another. Both legally and morally individuals and governments have no compunction about changing the rules at any time....
—David Rearwin
The Asia Business Book

This exercise is a brief introduction to the second of the four building blocks, personal versus societal responsibility. The two poles of this dimension, universalism and particularism, will be defined in the exercise immediately following this one.

You are riding in a car driven by a close friend when he hits a pedestrian. There are no other witnesses and the pedestrian is bruised but not badly hurt. The speed limit in this part of town is 20 miles an hour, but you noticed that your friend was driving 35. His lawyer tells you that if you will testify under oath that your friend was driving 20, he will suffer no serious consequences. (Adapted from Fons Trompenaars, *Riding the Waves of Culture.*)

Before reading further, circle yes or no in answer to this question: Would you testify that your friend was driving 20 miles an hour?

Yes   No

Percentage of Americans who said they would not: 96%
Percentage of Venezuelans who said they would not: 34%

What do you think accounts for the great difference between Venezuelan and American percentages? Now read the discussion on the following page for an explanation.

Discussion

There could be many explanations for the large difference here, but one of them almost certainly is the difference between being a universalist (as many Americans are) and a particularist (as many Venezuelans are). Universalists tend to feel that right is right, regardless of circumstances, while particularists tend to feel that circumstances (the person in trouble here is a friend) must be taken into account. This section of the workbook will explore these differences in greater detail.

Exercise 2.7

Universalist-Particularist

Back in Iran, a friend is a friend. You are brothers and you stick together no matter what.

—Iranian student in
John Fieg and John Blair
There Is a Difference

People in all cultures struggle with how to balance personal responsibilities to family, close friends, and colleagues (your ingroup), on the one hand, and responsibilities to society in general (composed of outgroups) on the other. In cases where these responsibilities conflict, people of different cultures often find themselves on opposing sides of this dichotomy.[1] The two poles, *universalism* and *particularism*, are defined below:

> *Universalism*: There are certain absolutes that apply across the board, regardless of circumstances or the particular situation. What is right is always right. Wherever possible, you should try to apply the same rules to everyone in like situations. To be fair is to treat everyone alike and not make exceptions for family, friends, or members of your ingroup. In general, ingroup/outgroup distinctions are minimized. Where possible, you should lay your personal feelings aside and look at situations objectively. While life isn't necessarily fair, you can make it more fair by treating everyone the same.

> *Particularism*: How you behave in a given situation depends on the circumstances. What is right in one situation may not be right in another. You treat family, friends, and your ingroups the best you can, and you let the rest of the world take care of itself. (*Their* ingroups will protect them.) One's ingroups and outgroups are clearly distinguished. There will always be exceptions made for certain people. To be fair is to

---

[1] The exercises in this building block owe a great deal to the excellent work of Fons Trompenaars and Charles Hampden-Turner on universalism and particularism. See Recommended Reading.

treat everyone as unique. In any case, no one expects life to be fair. Personal feelings should not be laid aside but rather relied upon.

No culture, of course, will be exclusively universalist or particularist—all cultures will have elements of both—but cultures do tend to be *more* one than the other. Due to personal differences (see exercise 1.3), individuals in a given culture could of course be anywhere along the continuum—though they are more likely to be on the same side as their culture—and may very well be at one spot in one set of circumstances and somewhere else in another. Personal differences notwithstanding, it is important to understand these two poles and the numerous cultural differences they account for.

The exercise which follows asks you to take the definitions of *universalism* and *particularism* presented above and apply them to specific examples of behavior. Below you will find a list of twelve items, each of which is more representative of one pole of this dimension than the other. Read each one and put a *U* next to those behaviors more consistent with universalism and a *P* next to those more consistent with particularism.

_____ 1.   A deal is a deal, whatever happens.

_____ 2.   You don't compromise on principles.

_____ 3.   Friends expect preferential treatment; friends protect friends.

_____ 4.   Consistency is desirable and possible.

_____ 5.   Justice is blind.

_____ 6.   Situational ethics prevail.

_____ 7.   Reason and logic prevail over feelings.

_____ 8.   Exceptions to the rule should be minimized.

_____ 9.   Principles are bent once in a while.

_____ 10.   Life is neat (as opposed to messy).

_____ 11.   There is a tendency to hire friends and associates.

_____ 12.   A deal is a deal, until circumstances change.

Suggested Answers

_U_ 1. Not taking circumstances into account is more universalist.

_U_ 2. Principles that apply across the board are more universalist.

_P_ 3. Ingroup members looking after each other is more particularist.

_U_ 4. Consistency is a core belief of universalism.

_U_ 5. This is universalist in the sense that the law should be the same for everyone.

_P_ 6. Taking circumstances into account is a hallmark of particularism.

_U_ 7. Reason is more consistent with objectivity, hence, universalism. Feelings are more consistent with subjectivity, hence particularism.

_U_ 8. Exceptions are by definition particularist.

_P_ 9. Principles are bent because you have to make exceptions.

_U_ 10. The universalist idea of being able to apply rules and principles across the board suggests that life is neater than it really is.

_P_ 11. Particularists favor their ingroup members.

_P_ 12. Circumstances count for much more in the particularist worldview.

Choices

This exercise introduces additional aspects of the universalist/ particularist building block and reviews some of those presented in exercise 2.7. It also asks you to think about your own preferences in this regard. Below you will find nine sets of paired statements, *a* and *b*. Read each pair and circle the number of the one which best describes the way you feel or the action you would take vis-à-vis that item. Please choose one even if you think that both alternatives are true or possible. For many of the examples, you might also be tempted to say, "It depends on the situation," which indeed it does. But choose anyway, without thinking too much!

_____ 1a. In hiring someone, I want to know about his or her technical skills and educational/professional background.

_____ 1b. In hiring, I want to know who the person's family and friends are, who will vouch for this person.

_____ 2a. In society, we should help those who are the neediest.

_____ 2b. In society, we should help the neediest of those who depend on us.

_____ 3a. I would be very hurt if my neighbor, a policeman, gave me a ticket for speeding.

_____ 3b. I would not expect my neighbor, the policeman, to jeopardize his job and not give me a speeding ticket.

_____ 4a. The courts should mediate conflicts.

_____ 4b. People should solve their own conflicts; it's embarrassing if people have to go to court.

Written contracts, keiyaka, are not as common in Japan as they are in the West, and even those contracts in Japan that are concluded in writing are not expected to be any more binding because of it.... To the Japanese a relationship is what holds agreements together.

—William Bohnaker
The Hollow Doll

_____ 5a. In general, people can be trusted.

_____ 5b. My closest associates can be trusted absolutely; everyone else is automatically suspect.

_____ 6a. Performance reviews should not take personal feelings into account.

_____ 6b. Performance reviews inevitably take personal feelings into account.

_____ 7a. You often have to make exceptions for people because of circumstances.

_____ 7b. Exceptions should be very rare; otherwise, you open the floodgates.

_____ 8a. Contracts aren't necessary between friends.

_____ 8b. Contracts guarantee that friends stay friends.

_____ 9a. What is ethical in a given situation depends on whom you are dealing with.

_____ 9b. Ethics are ethics no matter whom you are dealing with.

Now that you have circled your choices, read all the items again and decide which are more consistent with universalism (put a *U* in the blank) and which with particularism (put a *P*). Then check your answers. How many of your circled choices turned out to be universalist and how many particularist?

This exercise isn't scientific, of course, and doesn't "prove" anything about you. For one thing, all the items, as noted earlier, are taken out of context; you might very well select one alternative in one set of circumstances and the other in another set. Moreover, the choices you made for any given item may have more to do with some other aspect of your personality than your universalist or particularist tendencies. Even so, you have no doubt been given some food for thought and also been exposed to additional contexts in which this important concept operates and additional circumstances under which it might influence people's behavior.

Suggested Answers

Remember that an item marked *U* or *P* means only that the particular behavior tends to be *more* characteristic of a Universalist or a Particularist but is by no means exclusive to members of that category.

1a. *U*

1b. *P*

2a. *U*

2b. *P*

3a. *P*

3b. *U*

4a. *U*

4b. *P*

5a. *U*

5b. *P*

6a. *U*

6b. *P*

7a. *P*

7b. *U*

8a. *P*

8b. *U*

9a. *P*

9b. *U*

Exercise 2.9

What Would You Do?

Resting and gossiping under a tree, the medical aides would sometimes refuse treatment, saying the clinic was "closed for cleaning." It was a lie; no cleaning ever went on in that miserable mud-brick clinic. But having been appointed by relatives, the aides knew no work was required of them to keep their jobs.

—Peace Corps Volunteer
Senegal

Now that you have spent some time in the company of the universalist/particularist dichotomy, the moment has come to begin applying what you have learned. In this exercise, you will be presented with two situations where differences concerning this aspect of culture have caused an incident. These may be situations you have been in or can imagine being in. In any case, a successful resolution of each incident requires putting into practice what you know about this concept. Read each incident and jot down in the space below it what you would do or say if you were faced with this situation.

1. Between Friends

You are from a particularist culture, but you have emigrated recently to another country (a more universalist culture), where your good friend Mrs. Thompson lives and where you have been offered a job in the company where her husband works. You started work a few months ago, and everything went well until recently when you started having trouble with the day-care arrangements for your daughter. Because of this problem, you have been arriving an hour or more late to work at least twice a week. Yesterday Mr. Thompson, who manages the division you work in, complained to you about your tardiness and explained that you could not continue to come in late or you would get a reprimand in your personnel file.

You asked Mr. Thompson to do what he could to help you, but he explained that this is the standard policy and that to treat you differently would not be fair to the other employees. You are very hurt to be treated just like every other employee. After all, you are not just any employee; you are the friend of Mrs. Thompson and her husband. Friends make exceptions for friends, and other people understand this. You would certainly help them out if they were in trouble. What should you do now?

_____

_____

_____

2. Qualifications

You come from a universalist culture, but you live and work in a particularist one. You have been asked to fill a vacancy in the division you manage, and you have been reviewing the qualifications of various candidates. You intend to select Mr. Chu, a man who has worked his way up through the organization. He scores the highest on all the criteria against which the candidates are being measured, namely, education, work experience, technical skills, and knowledge of the job and the organization.

You are surprised and disappointed to learn that your boss, who has final approval, wants to hire the nephew of a certain well-connected family who may be in a position to steer a large government contract to your company. You believe this is very unfair to Mr. Chu and that it is not good in the long run for the company to hire someone who does not have the skills to do the job. What do you do?

_____

_____

_____

Discussion

Each of these incidents raises the same basic issue: What does a person on one side of the universalist/particularist divide do when working in a culture that is on the other side? What adjustments in his or her behavior and attitudes might be expected and appreciated by members of the other culture? People in these situations do not *have* to make these adjustments, of course, but they should at least understand the consequences of not doing so.

1. Between Friends

You may be hurt by Mr. Thompson's actions, but he actually believes he is behaving properly here and that you are the one who is being insensitive. In his universalist culture, friends would not ask for special favors, especially not in a work-related situation, where people who are friends outside of work are supposed to leave their personal feelings at the door. By asking for an exception, you are putting Mr. Thompson in a very difficult position, which is why he feels you're being insensitive.

As a particularist, you will have to think less in terms of ingroup/outgroup than you are used to and also to realize that universalists who try to treat everyone the same are only doing what they think is right—and are not slighting you. Remember that universalists who happen to be in your ingroup won't expect or even appreciate being given special treatment by you, and they certainly won't feel any obligation to give you special treatment. Remember also that acting like a universalist doesn't mean you have to treat everyone as if they were in your ingroup, as if they were special; it means treating people as if they were all in some kind of in-between group, neither in (deserving special attention) nor out (deserving none).

2. Qualifications

For universalists such as you to be effective in more particularist cultures, you must understand the importance of ingroups, that it is through ingroups and connections that things get done, and that people like Mr. Chu will of course understand and fully expect this. Indeed, Mr. Chu would probably be appalled to learn that you selected him for the job and thereby jeopardized an important contract that will keep everyone busy for several months. He certainly doesn't want to be responsible for that, nor should you want to be.

You have to remember that what you think of as fair, treating everyone the same, as if there were not ingroups and outgroups, will generally not be appreciated by particularists and will not win you any friends, including those you think you are defending against favoritism. They have long since accepted the reality of favoritism and play by those rules themselves.

You would be well advised to start distinguishing between people on the basis of whether they're in your ingroup or an outgroup, though this will not come naturally to you. You must remember that the people around you are doing this and that those who consider themselves members of your ingroup may very well feel free to make special claims on you (even as they extend special treatment to you). Remember, too, that people who consider themselves in the outgroup will neither extend you any particular courtesies nor expect or appreciate even-handed treatment from you. It will just confuse them.

Building Blocks 1 and 2

I feel my neighbors are rude, coming and asking for things from my garden. They believe I'm selfish, keeping my first harvest to myself.

—Peace Corps Volunteer
South Pacific

In this exercise, you will be comparing your culture and any other cultures you are interested in or need to know about—hereafter called "target cultures"—vis-à-vis the first two building blocks of culture: the concept of the self (individualist and collectivist) and personal versus societal responsibility (universalist and particularist). Once you see your culture's view of these important dimensions and the views of your target cultures, you will have identified major cultural differences that are a likely source of and explanation for common misunderstandings and misinterpretations.

The mechanism you will use to make these comparisons is the continua which appear on pages 50-51. You will see three different continua, one for the individualist/collectivist dimension and two for the universalist/particularist dimension (one called Personal versus Societal Responsibility and one called Subjective and Objective), with the poles or extremes of each topic described at either end. For each continuum, read the two descriptions and put a vertical line somewhere along the continuum—depending on which explanation you think more accurately describes the view of people from your culture in general on this issue. Not everyone will take the same view, of course, but try nevertheless to make a generalization about the perspective of a "typical" person from your culture on this topic.

For example, on the continuum marked Concept of Self, if you think the description under Individualist (left side) more accurately describes your culture's view or position on this matter, you will put your mark nearer to the left. For purposes of marking, think of each continuum as being divided into five segments, starting at the left:

extreme left	Put your mark here if the text at the left describes your culture very accurately.
halfway to the middle	Put your mark here if the text at the left is more or less accurate about your culture.
in the middle	Put your mark here if your culture is a true combination of the text at the right and left.
halfway from the middle	Put your mark here if the text on the right is more or less accurate about your culture.
extreme right	Put your mark here if the text at the right describes your culture very accurately.

After you have marked all three continua, you can then use the chart to compare your own culture with your target culture (or cultures) and identify important differences. You can do this in one of two ways:

1. You can give the chart to someone from the target culture and ask that person to complete it the same way you did, following the instructions given above.
2. You can consult the master list on page 52. This list locates a number of cultures or cultural groupings on the chart.

What do these marks mean? While these are all generalizations and not necessarily predictive of what individuals in any given culture might think, each mark represents how the people in that culture in general feel about that item on the continuum. More precisely, the marks indicate

- what the people in that culture think of as natural, normal, right, and good;
- how these people assume everyone feels about these issues; and
- which perspective these people use to interpret and judge the behavior of others (including you).

Where there is a wide gap between your mark and that of someone from the target culture, you can assume that you and that person may not see eye to eye on this matter. He or she may think your behavior or attitude is strange or surprising, and you may think the same about that person. And each of you is more likely to misinterpret or misunderstand the actions of the other in certain situations.

This doesn't mean that the two of you will never understand each other or be able to live or work together successfully, but it does mean that you may have very little intuitive understanding of each other with regard to this particular item. In other words, each of you will have to make some effort and exercise patience in trying to understand the other.

Finally, remember that context determines everything in human interaction. Nothing happens "in general"; things only happen in context, in specific circumstances. And depending on those circumstances, the individualist/collectivist or universalist/particularist tendencies of a person may or may not play a role, or at least not a deciding role, in any particular interaction. But they are always there as a potential, waiting for an opportunity to show themselves.

Concept of Self

Individualist

The self is the smallest unit of survival; looking out for one's self protects others; personal fulfillment is the greatest good; independence and self-reliance are highly valued; children are taught to stand on their own two feet; workers don't mind individual recognition; one's identity is personal and individual, not a function of one's membership or role in a group.

Collectivist

The primary group, usually the family, is the smallest unit of survival; looking out for others protects one's self; group harmony is the greatest good; children are taught to depend on others, who in turn can always depend on them; employees don't like to stand out, they prefer group/team recognition; identity is a function of one's membership/role in a primary group.

Personal versus Societal Responsibility

|———————|———————|———————|———————|

Universalist

What's right is always right; there are absolutes which apply across the board; the law is the law no matter who one is, there should be no exceptions; consistency is important; "fair" means treating everyone the same and one should try to make life fair.

Particularist

There are no absolutes; what's right depends on the circumstances; there must always be exceptions (for ingroup members); consistency is not possible (life isn't that neat); "fair" means treating everyone uniquely and no one expects life to be fair.

Subjective and Objective

|———————|———————|———————|———————|

Logic of the Head

Favoritism is frowned upon; people should not let personal feelings intrude into or affect workplace/professional decisions; friends don't expect friends to cover for them; people succeed because of what they do, not whom they know; to be objective is a positive thing, something to strive for.

Logic of the Heart

Favoritism is the norm; since the system isn't fair, people have to look out for their ingroup; whom you know, connections, are more important than performance; friends expect—and provide— preferential treatment; one can't and shouldn't leave personal feelings out of professional dealings.

Position of Selected Cultures

A number of cultures or cultural groupings have been selected for inclusion on this chart. The positions given here reflect either where nationals of these countries/regions have consistently placed themselves on this chart in numerous workshops and training seminars given by the author or where the author has placed these cultures after consulting various surveys and studies in the literature of the intercultural field. Remember that these placements are approximations and that they indicate the position of a culture as a whole on these matters, not of individuals. Even then, it's possible the reader may not agree with where his or her culture has been placed or even where other cultures have been placed. The best way to use these continuum charts is not to take our word for any of this, but to hand them to a person from another culture and let that individual speak for his or her own society. If any of your target cultures do not appear on this chart, you may be able to infer their position by noting the placement of a similar culture.

Concept of Self

| US | | UK F G | | R
I, S | | J | ME M A | | SEA
C |

Individualist — Collectivist

Personal versus Societal Responsibility

| US
G | UK | | | J | F | R
S | I, M
SEA | A, C
ME |

Universalist — Particularist

Subjective and Objective

| US
G | UK | | | J | | F | R
S | I, M
SEA | A, C
ME |

Logic of the Head — Logic of the Heart

A—Africa C—China F—France G—Germany I—India J—Japan
M—Mexico ME—Middle East R—Russia S—Spain
SEA—Southeast Asia UK—United Kingdom US—United States

CHAPTER 2

Service with a Smile

This exercise is a brief introduction to the third building block of culture, the concept of time. The two poles of this dimension, monochronic and polychronic, will be defined in the exercise which immediately follows this one.

Below you will find a picture of a shopkeeper standing behind the counter in his shop. Imagine that there are six patrons in this shop, all ready to be checked out. How should these six people arrange themselves vis-à-vis each other? Using circles to represent the patrons, draw in your answer.

Long delays no longer mattered. The threat of passing time was an idea alien to them. So what if it passed, it was a gift, like life and energy and speech, to be spent lavishly on those around them.
—Mary Cole
Dirtroads: Footloose in Africa

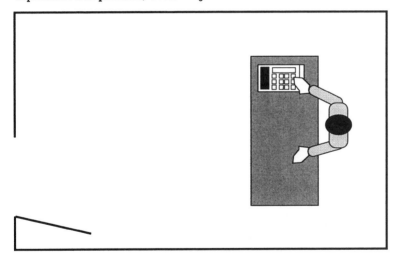

Now turn to the next page to see how respondents from a monochronic and a polychronic culture answered this question.

Discussion

Standing in a line is more characteristic of monochronic cultures, where people expect to be waited on one at a time and in order of arrival. In polychronic cultures, people expect to be waited on en masse and often do not stand in a neat line.

Drawing from Monochronic Respondents

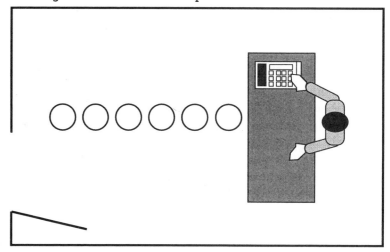

Drawing from Polychronic Respondents

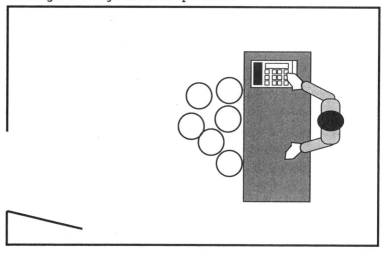

Monochronic–Polychronic

Another of the ways in which cultures differ is in how people conceive of and handle time and how their concept of time affects their interactions with each other.[1] The two poles of this building block, *monochronic* and *polychronic* time, are defined below.

Danish punctuality would result in hypertension in Greece.
—Max Messmer
Staffing Europe

> *Monochronic*: Time is a commodity; it is quantifiable and there is a limited amount of it. Therefore, it is necessary to use time wisely and not waste it. There is a premium on efficiency, hence a sense of urgency in many matters. Time is the given and people are the variable; the needs of people are adjusted to suit the demands of time (schedules, deadlines, etc.). It is considered most efficient to do one thing at a time or wait on one person at a time. As far as possible, you shouldn't let circumstances, unforeseen events, interfere with your plans. Interruptions are a nuisance.

> *Polychronic*: Time is limitless and not quantifiable. There is always more time, and people are never too busy. Time is the servant and tool of people and is adjusted to suit the needs of people. Schedules and deadlines often get changed. People may have to do several things simultaneously, as required by circumstances. It's not necessary to finish one thing before starting another, nor to finish your business with one person before starting in with another. You always have to take circumstances into account and make adjustments. Strictly speaking, there's no such thing as an interruption.

---

[1] The exercises in this building block owe a great debt to the groundbreaking work of Edward T. Hall. See Recommended Reading.

Once again, bear in mind that no culture is going to be exclusively monochronic or polychronic, that all cultures will have elements of both poles. But cultures do tend to be *more* one way than the other. Because of personal differences (see exercise 1.3), individuals within a given culture, of course, can be anywhere along the continuum and may very well be at one spot in one set of circumstances and somewhere else in another set. As a general rule, however, you should expect to find most individuals on the same side of the dichotomy as their culture as a whole.

The next exercise asks you to take the definitions of *monochronic* and *polychronic* presented above and apply them to specific examples of behavior. Below you will find a list of twelve items, each of which is more representative of one pole of this dimension than the other. Read each item and put an *M* next to those behaviors more consistent with monochronic time and a *P* next to those more consistent with polychronic.

_____ 1. Time is money.

_____ 2. To be late is rude.

_____ 3. The focus is on the task, getting the job done.

_____ 4. Having to wait is normal.

_____ 5. Interruptions are life.

_____ 6. Plans are fixed, once they are agreed upon.

_____ 7. The focus is on the person, establishing a relation-ship.

_____ 8. Everything depends on the circumstances.

_____ 9. People follow an internal clock.

_____ 10. Plans are always changing.

_____ 11. Having to wait is an insult.

_____ 12. People are sometimes too busy.

Suggested Answers

_M_ 1. In polychronic cultures, time is merely time.

_M_ 2. The concept of being late implies schedules and an imposition of structure upon time, which are characteristic of monochronic cultures.

_M_ 3. Monochronic cultures are organized around tasks.

_P_ 4. It is understood that people can't always control events to the extent that they or the other party will always be on time.

_P_ 5. Events often overlap.

_M_ 6. Monochronic cultures try not to take circumstances into account.

_P_ 7. People come first in polychronic cultures.

_P_ 8. You can't structure life, as hard as you may try.

_P_ 9. Polychronic types try to follow their feelings rather than the dictates of some external structure.

_P_ 10. Life is like that; you can never know what's going to happen, and depending on what happens, plans may have to change.

_M_ 11. Being on time is an important value, so being late (making someone wait) is frowned upon.

_M_ 12. People may not have enough time (but in polychronic cultures there is always enough time).

Exercise 2.12

Choices

An Australian man once visited the island and asked me when the stores were open, since it was afternoon and he hadn't seen a store open yet. Taken aback at what seemed a stupid question, I told him the obvious truth, "They're open when their doors are open." When I walked away I realized it was a question I would have asked myself when I first arrived on Fiji.

—Peace Corps Volunteer
Fiji

This exercise introduces additional aspects of the monochronic/polychronic building block and reviews some of those from exercise 2.11. It also asks you to think about your own tendencies regarding time. Below you will find ten sets of paired statements, *a* and *b*. Read each pair and circle letter *a* or *b*, whichever best describes the way you feel or the action you would take vis-à-vis that item. Please choose one even if you think the two alternatives are not mutually exclusive, in other words, that both are true or possible. For many of the examples, you might also be tempted to say, "It depends on the situation," which indeed it does. But choose anyway, without thinking too much!

_____ 1a. People should stand in line so they can be waited on one at a time.

_____ 1b. There's no need to stand in line, since people will be waited on as they are ready for service.

_____ 2a. Interruptions can usually not be avoided and are often quite beneficial.

_____ 2b. Interruptions should be avoided wherever possible; they are inefficient.

_____ 3a. It's more efficient if you do one thing at a time.

_____ 3b. You can get just as much done working on two or three things at the same time.

_____ 4a. It's more important to complete the transaction (if a meeting has gone beyond the scheduled time).

_____ 4b. It's more important to stick to the schedule (and continue the meeting at another time).

CHAPTER 2

_____ 5a. Unanticipated events are hard to accommodate and should be avoided when possible.

_____ 5b. Unexpected things happen all the time; that's life.

_____ 6a. You shouldn't take a telephone call or acknowledge a visitor when you are meeting with another person.

_____ 6b. It would be rude not to take a phone call or to ignore a visitor who drops by.

_____ 7a. You shouldn't take deadlines too seriously; anything can happen. What's a deadline between friends?

_____ 7b. Deadlines are like a promise; many other things depend on them, so they should not be treated lightly.

_____ 8a. It's important, in a meeting or a conversation, not to become distracted or digress. You should stick to the agenda.

_____ 8b. Digressions and distractions are inevitable. An agenda is just a piece of paper.

_____ 9a. You're never too busy to see someone; he or she would never understand if turned away.

_____ 9b. Sometimes you're just too busy to see people; they will understand.

_____ 10a. Personal talk is part of the job.

_____ 10b. Personal talk should be saved for after hours or during lunch.

Now that you have circled your choices, read all the pairs again and decide which are more consistent with monochronic time (put an *M* in the blank) and which with polychronic (put a *P*). Then check your answers. How many of your circled choices turned out to be monochronic and how many polychronic?

This exercise isn't scientific, of course, and doesn't "prove" anything about you. For one thing, all the items, as noted earlier, are taken out of context; you might very well select one alternative in one set of circumstances and the opposite in another. Moreover, the choices you made for any given item may have more to do with some other aspect of your personality than your monochronic or polychronic tendencies. Even so, you have no doubt been given some food for thought and also been exposed to additional contexts in which this important concept operates and additional circumstances under which it might influence people's behavior.

Suggested Answers

Remember that an item marked *M* or *P* means only that the particular behavior tends to be *more* characteristic of Monochronic people or Polychronic people but is by no means exclusive to members of that category.

 1a. *M*

 1b. *P*

 2a. *P*

 2b. *M*

 3a. *M*

 3b. *P*

 4a. *P*

 4b. *M*

 5a. *M*

 5b. *P*

 6a. *M*

 6b. *P*

 7a. *P*

 7b. *M*

 8a. *M*

 8b. *P*

 9a. *P*

 9b. *M*

10a. *P*

10b. *M*

What Would You Do?

A firm may say, "Yes, your shipment will be ready on Tuesday." You arrive on Tuesday to pick it up but find it is not ready. No one is upset or embarrassed.... Time commitments [in Mexico] are considered desirable objectives but not binding promises.

—Eva Kras
Management in Two Cultures

Now that you are familiar with the monochronic/polychronic dichotomy, the time has come to begin applying what you have learned. In this exercise, you will be presented with two situations where differences concerning this aspect of culture have caused an incident. These may be situations you have been in or can imagine being in. Regardless, a successful resolution of each incident requires putting into practice what you know about the monochronic/polychronic dichotomy. Read each incident and jot down in the space below it what you would do or say if you were faced with this situation.

1. Efficiency

You live in a polychronic culture. One of your colleagues is an immigrant from a monochronic culture and he is having problems adjusting to what he calls "unprofessionalism" in the workplace. He complains about how inefficient people are: they don't come to meetings on time; they come very late to appointments with him or they make him wait a long time when he has an appointment with them; when he is meeting with someone, that person will take telephone calls or talk to people who drop by and interrupt the conversation. "This is not the way to do business," he told you yesterday. Apparently he has complained to other people in your office as well, for just today some of them have come to you to complain about *him*. You are his closest friend in the office. What should you do?

_____

_____

_____

2. Caregiver

Yours is a monochronic culture. A nurse in an elderly-care home where you are the nursing supervisor comes from a more polychronic society, and her works habits are beginning to bother a lot of people, including several physicians and numerous residents. The latter complain that she is always late for her tasks, whether it's bathing them, helping them to the toilet, or taking them down to the dining room at mealtime. They say she's too friendly, by which they mean she spends too much time chatting with people (who nevertheless appreciate it a lot), and this puts her behind schedule. Physicians and other nurses complain that she's late to meetings and often reports late to work, which means someone on the shift before hers has to stay on until she arrives. Everyone likes this woman—she's outgoing and very compassionate—but she can be exasperating when it comes to managing her time. What's your next move?

_____

_____

_____

Discussion

Each of these incidents raises the same basic issue: What does a person on one side of the monochronic/polychronic divide do when working with a person or in a culture that is on the other side? What adjustments in his or her behavior and attitudes might be expected and appreciated by members of the other culture? People in these situations do not *have* to make these adjustments, of course, but they should at least understand the consequences of not doing so.

1. Efficiency

Your task here is to advise a monochronic person how to get along in a polychronic workplace. The first thing he needs to understand, of course, is that time is simply looked at differently in polychronic cultures and that ignoring people, not schedules, is the greater sin. Next, you might gently remind him that whatever he may think of such norms, he himself is now being judged by polychronic, not monochronic, standards. At the very least, this should sober him a bit.

Next you might encourage him to try to behave in those very ways he currently finds so frustrating. He himself should try coming later to meetings, which means he will arrive when everyone else does (and get a lot done back at his desk during the half hour he would have spent angrily waiting alone in the meeting room); he should feel free to take phone calls or chat with passersby when he is meeting with people, for they will expect and understand such behavior; and he too can feel free to make people wait for him if he has some business to attend to at an appointed hour.

The hardest thing, of course, will be getting him to believe that other people think all these behaviors are actually efficient. You may never get him to that point, but you might jolt him out of his certainty by asking him how efficient it is to insist on being monochronic in a polychronic world!

2. Caregiver

Our polychronic nurse doesn't realize she's polychronic, of course, much less that her polychronic behaviors are neither expected nor appreciated in the culture she has ended up in. Your first step, then, is to describe the monochronic worldview to her so that she has an opportunity to put her behavior in context. This doesn't mean she will become monochronic on the spot, but it does mean she will begin to understand better how she is perceived by the residents and staff.

You'll need to explain that meetings and appointments start on time (and that in this culture on time means at the hour given, not twenty minutes later), that things are somewhat driven by the clock, and that she will be evaluated in part on her promptness. You need not pull your punches here, for it is not fair to this woman to protect her from the consequences of her actions. She doesn't have to like the monochronic worldview, but she certainly needs to know about it and to understand the consequences of not modifying her behavior accordingly.

If she wants to spend more time with the residents, invite her to do so when she is off duty or when she has free time during the day.

Exercise 2.14

Who's in Charge Here?

So the people did get a new lagoon. They got it the same way they got their light plant that didn't work and their dock that stood high and dry at low tide: by sitting on their haunches and doing nothing. Some irrational part of me hoped that the rains would not come and that the lagoon would sit there forever... completely dry.

—Moritz Thomsen
Living Poor

This exercise is a brief introduction to the last of the four building blocks, the locus of control. The two poles of this dimension, internal and external locus, will be defined in the exercise immediately following this one.

Which of the following two statements do you most agree with? Circle one.

A. What happens to me is my own doing.

B. Sometimes I feel I don't have control over the direction my life is taking.

Percentage of Americans who chose A =   89%
Percentage of Chinese who chose A =   35%

What do you think accounts for the difference between American and Chinese answers? Now read the discussion on the following page for an explanation.

Discussion

There could be many explanations, but one almost certainly is the fact that many Americans believe in the power of the individual to prevail against all obstacles. There is nothing people cannot do or become if they want it badly enough and are willing to make the effort. This notion is best exemplified in the classic American expression: "Where there is a will there's a way."

In Chinese culture, many people believe that while you can shape your life to some extent, certain external forces beyond your control also play an important part. What happens to you in life is not entirely in your hands.

Exercise 2.15

Internal–External

Americans ignore history....
They believe in the future as if
it were a religion; they believe
that there is nothing they can-
not accomplish, that solutions
wait somewhere for all prob-
lems, like brides.
—Frances Fitzgerald
Fire in the Lake

Cultures differ greatly in their view of the individual's place vis-
à-vis the external world, especially on the question of to what
degree human beings can control or manipulate forces outside
themselves and thereby shape their own destiny. While all cultures believe that certain things happen outside of one's control, they differ as to what extent they believe this and on how
much one can do in response. The two poles of this dimension,
internal and *external*, are defined below.

> *Internal*: The locus of control is largely internal, within
> the individual. There are very few givens in life, few
> things or circumstances which have to be accepted as
> they are and cannot be changed. There are no limits
> on what you can do or become, so long as you set
> your mind to it and make the necessary effort. Your
> success is your own achievement. You are responsible
> for what happens to you. Life is what you do; hence,
> these represent more activist cultures.

> *External*: The locus of control is largely external to
> the individual. Some things in life are predetermined,
> built into the nature of things. There are limits be-
> yond which one cannot go and certain givens that
> cannot be changed and must be accepted. ("That's
> just the way things are.") Your success is a combina-
> tion of your effort and your good fortune. Life is in
> large part what happens to you; thus, these repre-
> sent more fatalist cultures.

Once again, bear in mind that no culture is going to be
exclusively internal or external, that all cultures will have elements of both poles. But cultures do tend to be *more* one way
than the other. Because of personal differences (see exercise

1.3), individuals in a given culture could of course be anywhere along the continuum and may very well be at one location in one set of circumstances and somewhere else in another. As a general rule, however, you should expect to find most individuals on the same side of the dichotomy as their culture as a whole.

The next exercise asks you to take the definitions of *internal* and *external* locus of control presented above and apply them to specific examples of behavior. Below you will find a list of twelve items, each of which is more representative of one pole of this dimension than the other. Read each one and put an *I* next to those behaviors more consistent with an internal orientation to control and an *E* next to those more consistent with an external locus.

_____ 1. The laws of nature can be discovered and manipulated.

_____ 2. Progress is inevitable.

_____ 3. Every problem has a solution.

_____ 4. Some things are a matter of luck or chance.

_____ 5. Where there's a will, there's a way.

_____ 6. Unhappiness is your own fault.

_____ 7. There is nothing automatic about progress.

_____ 8. The laws of nature are ultimately unknowable and cannot be manipulated.

_____ 9. You make your own luck.

_____ 10. Some problems do not have solutions.

_____ 11. Where there's a will, there may or may not be a way.

_____ 12. Unhappiness is a natural part of life.

Suggested Answers

_I_   1.   Nature, therefore, does not need to be accepted as it is.

_I_   2.   Progress is inevitable if it is within our control; if it weren't within our control, we couldn't say whether it was inevitable or not.

_I_   3.   This implies that we can figure everything out, that nothing is beyond our grasp.

_E_   4.   Luck or chance are hallmarks of the external locus worldview.

_I_   5.   This means everything depends upon individual motivation, not external factors.

_I_   6.   If we're in control, we can do what it takes to be happy.

_E_   7.   We would think this if we didn't feel we were ultimately in charge.

_E_   8.   In other words, there are factors and forces beyond our control.

_I_   9.   If we're in control, we make things happen.

_E_ 10.   Some problems are beyond our ability to figure out.

_E_ 11.   Willing something is not the same as making it happen; there could be other factors involved.

_E_ 12.   If there are things we have no control over, we are naturally susceptible to being unhappy.

Choices

This exercise introduces additional aspects of the locus of control building block and reviews some of those presented in exercise 2.15. It also asks you to think about your own assumptions about this matter. Below you will find eight sets of paired statements, *a* and *b*. Read each pair and circle letter *a* or *b,* whichever best describes the way you feel or the action you would take vis-à-vis that item. Please choose one even if you think the two alternatives are not mutually exclusive, in other words, that both are true or possible. For many of the examples, you might also be tempted to say, "It depends on the situation," which indeed it does. But choose anyway, without thinking too much!

Caution does not avert the decree of fate.
—Southern Arabian proverb

_____ 1a. I tend to be an optimist, to take a positive view of life.

_____ 1b. I tend to be a realist, to see life as neither better nor worse than it is.

_____ 2a. If I'm unhappy, I should do something about it.

_____ 2b. Nothing's wrong if I'm unhappy; it's just part of life's ups and downs.

_____ 3a. The external world is complex, dynamic, and mysterious. It cannot ultimately be understood or manipulated.

_____ 3b. The external world is a mechanism like other mechanisms; its workings can be discovered, predicted, even manipulated.

_____ 4a. If I try hard enough and want something badly enough, there is nothing to stop me from getting what I want.

_____ 4b. Some things are beyond my reach, no matter what I do.

_____ 5a. If a friend is depressed, there is no need for me to do anything.

_____ 5b. If a friend is depressed, I try to cheer him/her up.

_____ 6a. There is a solution for every problem, if you look hard enough.

_____ 6b. Some problems don't have a solution.

_____ 7a. I tend to be a stoic.

_____ 7b. I tend to be proactive and a doer.

_____ 8a. My success is a personal achievement.

_____ 8b. My success is my good fortune.

Now that you have circled your choices, read all the items again and decide which are more consistent with an internal locus of control (put an _I_ in the blank) and which with an external orientation (put an _E_). Then check your answers. How many of your circled choices turned out to be internal and how many external?

This exercise isn't scientific, of course, and doesn't "prove" anything about you. For one thing, all the items, as noted earlier, are taken out of context; you might very well select one alternative in one set of circumstances and the opposite one in another. Moreover, the choices you made for any given item may have more to do with some other aspect of your personality than your internal or external tendencies. Even so, you have no doubt been given some food for thought and also been exposed to additional contexts in which this important concept operates and additional circumstances under which it might influence people's behavior.

Suggested Answers

Remember that an item marked *I* or *E* means only that the particular behavior tends to be *more* characteristic of individuals who believe in an Internal or an External locus of control but is by no means exclusive to members of that category.

1a. *I*

1b. *E*

2a. *I*

2b. *E*

3a. *E*

3b. *I*

4a. *I*

4b. *E*

5a. *E*

5b. *I*

6a. *I*

6b. *E*

7a. *E*

7b. *I*

8a. *I*

8b. *E*

What Would You Do?

"The rains will come when it's time for them to come," I was told. And the people will wait for them. If the rains don't come this year, they will come next year, or they will come the year after, or maybe the year after that. And the people will be here waiting.

—Eddy L. Harris
Native Stranger

Now that you are familiar with the internal/external control dichotomy, the time has come to begin applying what you have learned. In this exercise, you will be presented with two situations where differences concerning this aspect of culture have caused a problem. These may be situations you have been in or can imagine being in. Whatever the case, a successful resolution of each incident requires putting into practice what you know about the concept of the locus of control. Read each incident and jot down in the space below it what you would do or say if you were faced with this situation.

1. The Bright Side

You are an activist working in a fatalistic society. The company you work for has hired you to help its expand its business and get new customers. You have designed a campaign that should result in a 5 percent increase in market share in six months if you can get all the resources you need. You have been spending the last few weeks drumming up enthusiasm and support for your master plan, but to be honest, colleagues and upper management haven't been responding the way you would like. They're quite pessimistic about your estimates; to get that kind of increase, they say, will take a lot longer than six months. "Things just don't happen that fast here," you were told by one manager. Your reply was that things can happen as fast (or slow) as people want them to; they just have to make the necessary effort.

Everyone seems to have a reason why the plan won't work, why the potential stumbling blocks are more serious than you think. You realize there will be some obstacles, of course, but you have faced these kinds of obstacles before and know that if people rise to the occasion, they can overcome them. If the company isn't serious, however, if it doesn't commit the personnel and other resources required, this expansion won't happen in six years, much less six months.

You're starting to doubt whether these people are really committed to this effort or if they're just making the right noises. And you weren't encouraged today when your boss told you that some department heads have been complaining about the demands you're making of them, saying that you're not being very realistic. What should you do?

_____

_____

_____

2. It Wasn't Meant to Be

You work for an advertising firm in an activist culture to which you emigrated two years ago. While you like your adopted homeland very much, it has been difficult to adjust your more fatalist inclinations to the prevailing mindset, especially at work. You work as hard as anyone else, but you have been accused of giving up on prospective new accounts when you might have won them with more effort. You feel that after you have pitched to and courted clients for a certain period, the rest is up to them, that beyond a certain point there's nothing more you can do. You have even been accused of being defeatist for saying that certain goals were unrealistic.

Last week your boss called you in for your yearly performance review. He pointed out that you needed to be more aggressive in pursuing business and not be so eager to adopt a wait-and-see stance after you have pitched to clients. "Things happen because you make them happen," he said, "not because they're *meant* to happen." You don't necessarily agree, but you obviously need to adjust your style if you're going to succeed in this organization. What can you do to be more effective in this environment?

_____

_____

_____

Discussion

Each of these incidents raises the same basic issue: What does an individual from one end of the continuum of this building block do when working in a culture that is at the other end? What adjustments in his/her behavior and attitudes might be expected and appreciated by members of such a culture? Individuals in these situations do not *have* to make any such adjustments, of course, but they should at least consider the possibility—as well as the consequences of not doing so.

1. The Bright Side

Coming from an activist culture and believing as you do in an internal locus of control, you see getting things done as merely a function of people making the required effort. Your colleagues, on the other hand, look at the world and see a very different place, a place where even when people do all they can, certain things still may not happen—or may not happen until some other things are done. And these other things may be beyond anyone's control. This doesn't mean you can't get the job done here, but it may very well mean, as these people keep telling you, that it's going to take longer than you think.

Your view of the stumbling blocks is likewise colored by your culture's sense of the individual being in control. If there are obstacles, you just take whatever steps may be needed to vanquish them. Your colleagues probably believe that obstacles can ultimately be vanquished too, but once again they calculate into the equation that doing so will require a combination of one's own efforts and the efforts of people or forces outside one's control. These outside factors, needless to say, will proceed at their own pace; you can and should try to nudge them along, but there are limits to what you can do.

Your strategy here should be to calm down; do all you can, encourage others to do all they can, even be a bit of a nuisance if you like. But don't be too attached to your timetable. Meanwhile, both you and your colleagues will be a lot happier if you stop judging how much people want this expansion by the amount of effort they're willing to put into it.

2. It Wasn't Meant to Be

You should remember that people who believe in an internal locus of control will probably come across as unrealistic to you. At the same time, you will come across as defeatist to them unless you adopt (publicly, at least) a generally positive, can-do attitude. Optimism is a natural attitude for people who believe deeply in their ability to "make things happen," as your boss has put it. In such cultures, anyone who suggests that there may be more to getting things done than a positive attitude and lots of effort, who believes as you do that factors beyond your control may also play a role, runs the risk of appearing to be making excuses for not working hard enough.

Your approach, then, might be to act a little less like a realist, support goals you think may be unattainable—what does it hurt to set one's sights a little too high?—and especially to pursue clients further than you would in your own culture. You might think these clients will be put off by your tenacity, but in some cases they might actually be impressed by your persistence, or, as they might see it, by your confidence in your company.

Above all, remember that in cultures where the prevailing belief is that people make things happen, there is always more you can do in pursuit of any goal. Even if those things don't work, even if you know those things aren't going to work, you should never appear to be giving up.

Review Exercise

Building Blocks 3 and 4

In this second continuum exercise, you will be comparing your own and target cultures vis-à-vis the third and fourth building blocks of culture: the concept of time (monochronic/polychronic) and the locus of control (internal/external). Once you see your culture's view of these important dimensions and the view of your target cultures, you will have identified major cultural differences that are a likely source of and explanation for common misunderstandings and misinterpretations.

Once again, you will use the continuum technique to make these comparisons (see pages 80-81). You will see three different continua, two for monochronic/polychronic (one called Concept of Time and one called Time and Other People) and one for internal/external Locus of Control, with the poles or extremes of each topic described at either end. For each continuum, read the two descriptions and put a vertical line somewhere along the continuum, depending on which explanation you think more accurately describes the view of people from your culture in general on this issue. Not everyone will take the same view, of course, but try nevertheless to make a generalization about the position of a "typical" person from your culture on this topic.

For example, on the continuum marked Concept of Time, if you think the description under Monochronic (left side) more accurately describes your culture's position on this matter, you will put your mark nearer to the left. As in the Review Exercise on pages 48-52, for purposes of marking, think of each continuum as being divided into five segments, starting at the left:

extreme left	Put your mark here if the text at the left describes your culture very accurately.
halfway to the middle	Put your mark here if the text at the left is more or less accurate about your culture.
in the middle	Put your mark here if your culture is a true combination of the text at the right and left.
halfway from the middle	Put your mark here if the text on the right is more or less accurate about your culture.
extreme right	Put your mark here if the text at the right describes your culture very accurately.

After you have marked all three continua, you can then use the chart to compare your own culture with your target culture (or cultures) and identify important differences. You can do this in one of two ways:

1. You can give the chart to someone from the target culture and ask that person to complete it the same way you did, following the instructions given above.
2. You can consult the master list on page 82. This list locates a number of cultures or cultural groupings on the chart.

What do these marks mean? While these are all generalizations and therefore not predictive of what individuals in any given culture might think, each mark represents how the people in that culture in general feel about that item on the continuum. More precisely, the marks indicate

- what the people in that culture think of as natural, normal, right, and good;
- how these people assume everyone feels about these issues; and
- which perspective these people use to interpret and judge the behavior of others (including you).

Where there is a wide gap between your mark and that of someone from the target culture, you can assume that you and that person may not see eye to eye on this matter. He or she may think your behavior or attitude is strange or surprising, and you may think the same about that person. And each of you is more likely to misinterpret or misunderstand the actions of the other in certain situations.

This doesn't mean that the two of you will never understand each other or be able to live or work together successfully, but it does mean that you may have very little intuitive understanding of each other with regard to this particular item. In other words, each of you will have to make some effort and exercise patience in trying to understand the other.

Finally, remember that context determines everything in human interaction. Nothing happens "in general"; things only happen in context, in specific circumstances. And depending on those circumstances, the monochronic/polychronic or internal/external control tendencies of a person may or may not play a role, or at least not a deciding role, in any particular interaction. But they are always there as a potential, waiting for an opportunity to show themselves.

Concept of Time

Monochronic

Time is a limited commodity; the needs of people are subservient to the demands of time; deadlines and schedules are sacred; plans are not easily changed; people may be too busy to see you; people live by an external clock.

Polychronic

Time is bent to meet the needs of people; there is always more time; schedules and deadlines are easily changed; plans are fluid; people always have time to see you; people live by an internal clock.

Time and Other People

One Thing at a Time

People do one thing at a time and finish one thing before starting another; people expect undivided attention; interruptions are to be avoided; to be late or kept waiting is rude; people stand in line; the goal is to stick to the schedule.

Many Things at Once

People may do several things at the same time and may split their attention between several people/tasks; to be late or kept waiting is okay; interruptions are part of life; people don't stand in line; the goal is to enjoy life.

Locus of Control

Internal

The locus of control is internal; fate has little or no importance; there are few givens in life, few things that can't be changed and must just be accepted; where there's a will, there's a way; one makes one's own luck; unhappiness is one's own fault; people tend to be optimistic; life is what you make it.

External

The locus of control is external; fate plays a major role; people believe they have limited control over their destiny/external events; many things in life must be accepted/can't be changed; success/lack of success is partly a result of good/bad fortune; people tend to be realistic/fatalistic; life is what happens to you.

Position of Selected Cultures

A number of cultures or cultural groupings have been selected for inclusion on this chart. The positions given here reflect either where nationals of these countries/regions have consistently placed themselves on this chart in numerous workshops and training seminars given by the author or where the author has placed these cultures after consulting various surveys and studies in the literature of the intercultural field. Remember that these placements are approximations and that they indicate the position of a culture as a whole on these matters, not of individuals. Even then, it's possible the reader may not agree with where his or her culture has been placed or even where other cultures have been placed. The best way to use these continuum charts is not to take our word for any of this but to hand them to a person from another culture and let that individual speak for his or her own society. If any of your target cultures do not appear on this chart, you may be able to infer their position by noting the placement of a similar culture.

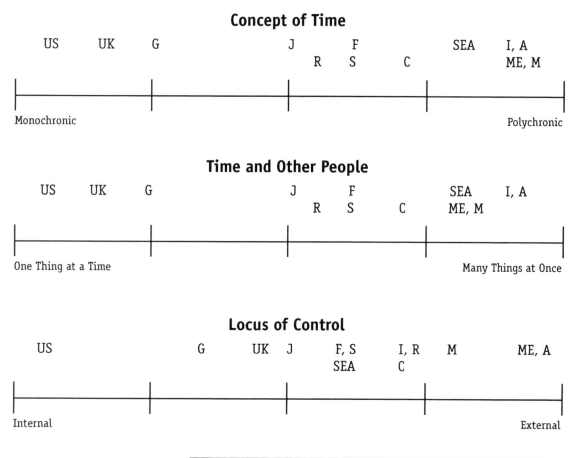

Concept of Time

US UK G J F SEA I, A
R S C ME, M

Monochronic — Polychronic

Time and Other People

US UK G J F SEA I, A
R S C ME, M

One Thing at a Time — Many Things at Once

Locus of Control

US G UK J F, S I, R M ME, A
SEA C

Internal — External

A—Africa C—China F—France G—Germany I—India J—Japan
M—Mexico ME—Middle East R—Russia S—Spain
SEA—Southeast Asia UK—United Kingdom US—United States

CHAPTER 2

Dialogues Revisited

Now that you have completed this chapter, reread the dialogues in the diagnostic exercise (exercise 2.1) on pages 21–22 to see whether you notice anything new in light of what you have learned about culture in the foregoing exercises. Then read the analyses below for a description of the cultural differences that were being illustrated in the dialogues. (It's possible you will have seen differences other than those described below.)

1. Near the Family

This dialogue illustrates a classic difference between the collectivist and individualist worldviews. Sharon, from an individualist culture, assumes that Fatima, now that she is about to finish college and go to work, will be living on her own. In Sharon's culture, after all, to live on one's own, to be independent and self-reliant, is the goal one prepares—and is prepared—for throughout one's formative years. Achieving that goal, symbolized by moving out of your parents' home and into your own residence, indicates that you are ready to take your place in the adult world.

It does in some cultures, anyway, but apparently not in Fatima's more collectivist culture. On the contrary, in cultures like Fatima's the goal you work toward during your youth is the ability to live easily and happily with your primary group, usually your immediate or extended family. You have become an adult in such cultures when you are able to take your rightful place in this ingroup and fulfill your various duties and responsibilities, whether as oldest son, married daughter, son-in-law, and so on.

In other words, Fatima isn't going to live near her family; she is, of course, going to live *with* her family, for now and for the foreseeable future.

2. Vacancy

There's a good reason why Luigi hasn't finished writing that job advertisement yet: advertising is a mighty poor way to fill a vacancy. After all, *anyone* can respond to an ad, and what company wants just anyone working for it? What you want is someone you can trust and rely on, someone from the right background, with the right values and the right style and manners. And it goes without saying that you don't *find* such people, you *know* them. Or someone you know knows them and can vouch for them—or so the thinking goes in Luigi's particularist culture.

Naturally, when Luigi suggests his niece Marta, a member of his ingroup, he expects that will solve the matter of the vacancy and make the advertisement unnecessary. Clearly, Luigi wouldn't risk the good name of his ingroup by recommending his niece if she weren't the right sort of person for the job, and since Marta *is* his niece, then he will know if she's the right sort of person. But unaccountably, Horst tells Luigi to ask Marta to *apply* for the job, implying that Marta will be subject to some other set of criteria.

For the more universalist Horst, there are such criteria: Is Marta the most technically qualified person available? She may be a nice young lady from a good family, but the bottom line is: Can she do the work? Does she have the skills and experience? Regardless of whom she is related to, she must be judged according to certain objective standards. This matters to Luigi too—he wouldn't have recommended the girl if she didn't have the necessary basic skills—but her relationship to Luigi and all that that implies (which isn't much as far as Horst is concerned) is what really qualifies her.

In universalist cultures, Luigi's approach smacks of favoritism at best and discrimination at worst—and is even illegal in some cases.

3. Helping Miss Thomas

This is a classic monochronic/polychronic incident. Miss Thomas, from a monochronic culture, expects to receive the undivided attention of the shopkeeper, Roberto, until she has finished her business. Then he will direct his attention to the next customer, who, meanwhile, is supposed to wait quietly in line until it is his or her turn to be served.

Or so things unfold in Miss Thomas's well-ordered monochronic world. But not, clearly, in Roberto's neck of the woods. Being polychronic, he greets all his customers as soon as they arrive (it would be impolite to ignore them) and proceeds to do the only courteous thing under the circumstances—wait on them all simultaneously. Miss Thomas may perceive this as service interrupted, but Roberto no doubt sees it as service expanded.

4. Out of Order

Here we have an activist and a fatalist squaring off in front of a broken elevator. Larisa apparently comes from a culture where the locus of control is internal, where the normal, instinctive response to something that is broken is either to fix it or to set in motion the chain of events that will result in its becoming fixed. Her cultural assumption is that the solution to this problem—and to any problem—lies in individual, personal action. One may or may not choose to take such action, of course, but there is no question that if one does, one can bring about the desired end.

Miranda inhabits a different world. While there are some things she believes she can affect by personal action, there are other things, all those under the sway of an external locus of control, which she cannot influence by any amount or kind of personal intervention. And one such thing, apparently, is this broken elevator. Hence her surprise at Larisa's attempts to get to the bottom of this problem ("Whom should we talk to?"), for this problem is clearly one where individual action cannot affect the outcome.

For Miranda, of course, who is also taken aback, there is ultimately no such category as individual action.

Styles of Communication

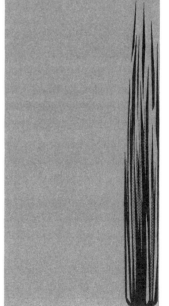

Communication, the sending and receiving of messages, is one of the most common of all human behaviors, playing a prominent role in nearly every interaction between two people. It should come as no suprise, then, that culture, a key factor in behavior, is likewise a key element in communication. What people say, how they say it, what they don't say—and especially what they *mean* by what they say—are all deeply affected by culture.

Edward T. Hall, one of the founders of the intercultural field, said that culture *is* communication. What he probably meant was that since so many of our waking hours are spent in one form of communication or another and culture is such a pervasive influence in communication, it's hard to tell where one leaves off and the other begins. Whether they are one and the same or not, culture and communication certainly make an attractive couple.

In the cross-cultural context, communication, like everything else, gets complicated. What words mean, what nonverbal behaviors mean, the meaning of what is not said or done—all of these modes of communication are used differently by people in different cultures. In the end, whether the message you send is the one that gets received and whether the message you receive is the one that was sent are no longer foregone conclusions.

Chapter 3

Every country has its way of saying things. The important thing is that which lies behind people's words.
—Freya Stark
The Journey's Echo

Exercise 3.1

Dialogues

If we listen to words merely, and give them our own habitual values, we are bound to go astray.

—Freya Stark
The Journey's Echo

You will begin your exploration of communication with another diagnostic exercise, once again in the form of dialogues. A dialogue, you will recall from exercise 2.1, is a brief conversation between people from two different cultures which illustrates one or more cultural differences. The dialogues which follow illustrate differences between direct and indirect styles of communication, the major theme of this chapter.

Your task here, as before, is to read each dialogue and try to identify the cultural difference. Remember that dialogues are deliberately written in such a way that this difference may not jump out at you—just as it is not always obvious to speakers in similar real-life conversations—but it is there for those who can see it. If you can't, don't worry; the information in the rest of this chapter will help you get to the bottom of the dialogues.

As noted earlier, you may feel that the speakers in these dialogues need not come from different cultures in order to have these conversations, that the misunderstanding or confusion could easily occur between two speakers from the same culture. That is entirely possible, of course; the point here is not that a cultural difference is the *only* explanation for these kinds of misunderstandings, but that when the two parties involved come from different cultures, it is always a possible explanation.

After you have tried to figure out the dialogues, you should go ahead and complete the other exercises in this chapter. Later, you will be asked to return to this exercise and reread these dialogues in light of what you will then know about styles of communication.

You will, incidentally, find the "answers" to these dialogues—an explanation of what was happening in each one—at the end of this chapter in the section called "Dialogues Revisited" (pages 123–126). While you might be tempted to read these answers now, before working the intervening exercises, you are strongly encouraged to hold off; if you curb your curiosity now and then reread the dialogues as recommended, you will have the distinct pleasure of figuring them out on your own!

1. A Call from Hari

MAGDA: I wonder where Hari is.

BOB: Oh, I forgot to tell you. He called.

MAGDA: He called?

BOB: Yes. He said he was too busy to come over in person.

MAGDA: But he always comes. And we have coffee together.

BOB: I know. He said he was sorry and he would try to come next week.

MAGDA: I'd better get over there and talk to him.

BOB: I'd wait until next week if I were you. He's really busy.

2. A Bit of a Nuisance

GITTI: How did it go with Arabella?

KARL: Much better than I expected.

GITTI: Did you explain everything to her?

KARL: Yes. I said that we were very sorry but we weren't going to be able to meet the deadline.

GITTI: What did she say?

KARL: She just said "That's a bit of a nuisance" and started talking about something else.

GITTI: That's a relief.

3. Saturday Shift

Ms. Jones: It looks like we're going to need some people to come in on Saturday.

Mr. Wu: I see.

Ms. Jones: Can you come in on Saturday?

Mr. Wu: Yes, I think so.

Ms. Jones: That'll be a great help.

Mr. Wu: Yes. Saturday's a special day, did you know?

Ms. Jones: How do you mean?

Mr. Wu: It's my son's birthday.

Ms. Jones: How nice. I hope you all enjoy it very much.

Mr. Wu: Thank you. I appreciate your understanding.

4. Rewrite

Susan: So, what did you think of my rewrite?

Yang: Ah yes, the rewrite. Generally tighter than the first draft, don't you think?

Susan: I do. Shall I send it down for printing, then?

Yang: It's up to you, really.

Direct and Indirect Communication

The dimension of communication on which cultures differ the most and the one affecting more aspects of the communication dynamic is the matter of directness. The differences between the two poles of this dimension, directness and indirectness, probably account for more cross-cultural misunderstanding than any other single factor.[1] These two poles are described below:

> *Indirect/High Context*: People in these cultures tend to infer, suggest, and imply rather than say things directly. At least that is how they appear to people from more direct/low-context cultures—though not, of course, to each other. These cultures tend to be more collectivist, where harmony and saving face are the greatest goods; hence, there is a natural tendency toward indirectness and away from confrontation. In collectivist cultures, ingroups are well established and members have an intuitive understanding of each other, in part because of shared experiences. This means that as a rule people don't need to spell things out or say very much to get their message across. This intuitive understanding is known as context, and in high-context cultures messages often don't even need words to be expressed; nonverbal communication may be enough, or the message may be expressed in terms of what is not said or done. The goal of most communication exchanges is preserving and strengthening the relationship with the other person.

Maintaining a peaceful, comfortable atmosphere is more important [to Koreans] than attaining immediate goals or telling the absolute truth. Koreans believe that to accomplish something while causing unhappiness or discomfort to individuals is to accomplish nothing at all.
—Sonja Vegdahl Hur and
Ben Seunghwa Hur
Culture Shock: Korea

---

[1] The important work of Edward T. Hall is a key source for all exercises dealing with the concept of high- and low-context cultures. See Recommended Reading.

Direct/Low Context: Direct cultures tend to be less collectivist and more individualist than indirect cultures, with less well-developed ingroups. People lead more independent lives and have fewer shared experiences; hence, there is less instinctive understanding of others. People need to spell things out and be more explicit, to say exactly what they mean rather than merely suggest or imply. There is less context, less that can be taken for granted. The spoken word carries most of the meaning; you should not read anything into what is not said or done. The goal of most communication exchanges is getting or giving information.

No culture uses the direct or indirect approach exclusively, but most cultures tend to be *more* one way than the other. Individuals within a given culture, of course, may be anywhere along the scale because of particular personal differences. As a general rule, though, you should expect to find most individuals on the same side of the divide as their culture as a whole.

The following exercise asks you to consider the definitions of *indirect/high-context* and *direct/low-context* communication styles as presented above and apply them to specific examples of behavior. Below you will find a list of twelve items, each of which is more representative of one pole of this dimension than the other. Read each item and put an *I* next to those behaviors more consistent with indirectness and a *D* next to those more consistent with directness.

_____ 1.   This is like the communication between siblings.

_____ 2.   This is like the communication between two casual acquaintances.

_____ 3.   People are reluctant to say no.

_____ 4.   You may have to read between the lines to understand what someone is saying.

_____ 5.   It's best to tell it like it is.

_____ 6.   Yes means yes.

_____ 7.   Yes means I hear you.

_____ 8.   There is no need to read between the lines.

_____ 9.   Who attends your meeting is an indication of how important you or the topic is.

_____ 10. Who attends your meeting is an indication of who is available to attend.

_____ 11. Silence may mean disapproval or dissatisfaction.

_____ 12. People tell you what they think you want to hear.

Suggested Answers

_I_ 1. Members of the same family usually have considerable shared experiences, hence more innate understanding. They can thus be more indirect with each other.

_D_ 2. Because they share less common understanding, they have to be more direct.

_I_ 3. This is more characteristic of collectivist cultures, which prize harmony and are therefore more indirect.

_I_ 4. Understatement is classic indirect style.

_D_ 5. Some people don't like what they call "beating around the bush."

_D_ 6. Direct communicators should be interpreted fairly literally.

_I_ 7. Since saying no may not be an option, yes is more of an automatic response, which may not mean very much.

_D_ 8. This is because the lines (the words) are the primary carrier of meaning.

_I_ 9. Where words are not the primary carrier of meaning, other methods are used to communicate the message.

_D_ 10. Where words are the primary carrier of the message, you don't read so much extra meaning into nonverbal behaviors.

_I_ 11. If saying no is impolite and saying yes might mislead, then saying nothing can be the polite way of saying no.

_I_ 12. This saves face and preserves harmony.

Comparing Communication Styles across Cultures

This exercise is similar to the two continuum exercises in chapter 2 (Review Exercises on pages 48 and 78). In this instance, you will be comparing the communication style of your culture with that of your target cultures. Once you see your own culture's communication norms and expectations and those of your target cultures, you will be able to identify major cultural differences, differences that are a likely source of and explanation for common misunderstandings and misinterpretations.

You will be using the continua on pages 97–98 to make these comparisons. There are three of these, with the poles or extremes of each topic described on opposite ends of the lines. For each continuum, read the two descriptions and put a vertical line somewhere along the continuum, depending on which explanation you think more accurately describes the view of people from your culture in general on this issue. Not everyone will take the same view, of course, but try nevertheless to make a generalization about the position of a "typical" person from your culture on this topic.

For example, on the continuum marked Degree of Directness, if you think the description under Direct (left side) more accurately describes your culture's position on this matter, you will put your mark nearer to the left. As you did in the previous continuum exercises, for purposes of marking, think of each continuum as being divided into five segments, starting at the left:

extreme left	Put your mark here if the text at the left describes your culture very accurately.
halfway to the middle	Put your mark here if the text at the left is more or less accurate about your culture.

The hardest thing to get in Europe is simplicity, people saying what they think and feel, openly and directly. It never happens.

—Stuart Miller
Understanding Europeans

in the middle   Put your mark here if your culture is a true combination of the text at the right and left.

halfway from the middle   Put your mark here if the text on the right is more or less accurate about your culture.

extreme right   Put your mark here if the text at the right describes your culture very accurately.

After you have marked all three continua, you can then use the chart to compare your own culture with your target culture (or cultures) and identify important differences. You can do this in one of two ways:

1. You can give the chart to someone from the target culture and ask him or her to complete it the same way you did, following the instructions given above.
2. You can consult the master list on pages 99-100. This list locates a number of cultures or cultural groupings on the chart.

What do these marks mean? While these are all generalizations and therefore not predictive of what individuals in any given culture might think, each mark represents how the people in that culture in general feel about that item on the continuum. More precisely, the marks indicate

- what the people in that culture think of as natural, normal, right, and good;
- how these people assume everyone feels about these issues; and
- which perspective these people use to interpret and judge the behavior of others (including you).

Where there is a wide gap between your mark and that of someone from the target culture, you can assume that you and that person communicate rather differently. He or she may think your style is quite strange or surprising, and you may think the same about that person's style. And each of you is more likely to misinterpret or misunderstand the messages being sent by the other.

This doesn't mean that the two of you will never understand each other or be able to live or work together successfully, but it does mean that you won't start out with a kind of mutual understanding. In other words, each of you will have to make some effort and exercise patience as you try to figure the other person out.

Finally, remember that context determines everything in human interaction. Nothing happens "in general"; things only happen in context, in specific circumstances. And depending on those circumstances, the tendencies of a person toward directness or indirectness may or may not play a role, or at least not a deciding role, in a particular interaction. But those cultural instincts are always there as a potential, waiting for an opportunity to show themselves.

Degree of Directness

Direct

People say what they mean and mean what they say; there is no need to read between the lines; it's best to tell it like it is; people are less likely to imply and more likely to say exactly what they are thinking; yes means yes.

Indirect

People don't always say what they mean or mean exactly what they say; you have to read between the lines; people are more likely to suggest or imply than to come out and say what they think; you can't always tell it like it is (what if that upsets the other person?); yes may mean maybe or even no.

Role of Context

|———————————|———————————|———————————|———————————|———————————|

Low Context

People are individualistic; ingroups are not as well developed as they are in high-context cultures and people spend less time in them, hence there are fewer shared experiences and less shared understanding; one has to spell things out and be explicit; words are the primary carriers of meaning; what is said is more important than what is not said.

High Context

People tend to be collectivistic; ingroups are strong and people spend a lot of time together, hence, there are more shared experiences and more common understanding than there are in low-context cultures; there is less need to spell things out; more is implicit; words are not always the primary carriers of meaning; what is not said may be more important than what is.

Importance of Face

|———————————|———————————|———————————|———————————|———————————|

Face Less Important

Telling the truth is more important than sparing someone's feelings; honesty is the best policy; it's okay to say no and to confront people; people don't worry much about saving face; getting/giving information efficiently is the primary goal of the communication exchange.

Face More Important

Preserving harmony and saving face are key concerns; the truth, if it threatens harmony or someone's face, should be adjusted; one says what one thinks the other person wants to hear; it's not always proper to say no, disagree, or confront (that disturbs harmony); preserving/strengthening the personal bond is the goal of the communication exchange.

Position of Selected Cultures

A number of cultures or cultural groupings have been selected for inclusion on this chart. The positions given here reflect either where nationals of these countries/regions have consistently placed themselves on this chart in numerous workshops and training seminars given by the author or where the author has placed these cultures after consulting various surveys and studies in the literature of the intercultural field. Remember that these placements are approximations and that they indicate the position of a culture as a whole on these matters, not of individuals. Even then, it's possible the reader may not agree with where his or her culture has been placed or even where other cultures have been placed. The best way to use these continuum charts is not to take our word for any of this but to hand them to a person from another culture and let that individual speak for his or her own society. If any of your target cultures do not appear on this chart, you may be able to infer their position by noting the placement of a similar culture.

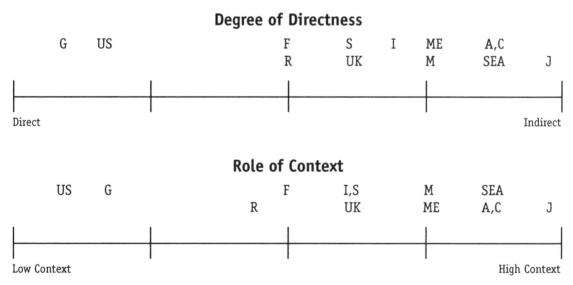

Degree of Directness

```
   G    US                    F      S    I   ME      A,C
                              R      UK        M       SEA      J
|---------------|-------------|-------------|-------------|
Direct                                                    Indirect
```

Role of Context

```
      US   G                   F     I,S        M      SEA
                          R          UK        ME      A,C      J
|---------------|-------------|-------------|-------------|
Low Context                                          High Context
```

3.3

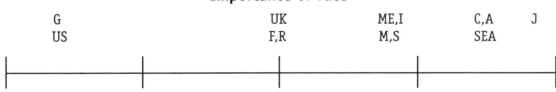

Importance of Face

G   UK   ME,I   C,A   J
US   F,R   M,S   SEA

Face Less Important   Face More Important

A—Africa   C—China   F—France   G—Germany   I—India   J—Japan
M—Mexico   ME—Middle East   R—Russia   S—Spain
SEA—Southeast Asia   UK—United Kingdom   US—United States

Communication Techniques

This chart presents a number of common communication techniques and shows how the different meanings attached to these techniques by direct and indirect communicators lead to inevitable misinterpretations and misunderstandings. For each number read the first three columns and then in the last column, on the right, write how you think each type of communicator would interpret the other when he or she uses this technique. The first one has been done for you as an example.

Khoo Ah Au liked Americans. Above all he found their personal relationships easy to read. His own people were always very careful not to give themselves away, to expose crude feelings about one another. Americans seemed not to care how much was understood by strangers. It was almost as if they enjoyed being transparent.

—Eric Ambler
Passage of Arms

Technique Used by Speaker	Meaning in a Direct Culture	Meaning in an Indirect Culture	Possible Misinterpretations
1. Understatement ("I have one small suggestion.")	Understatements are often taken literally; in this case, the listener would assume the speaker doesn't feel strongly about this matter.	This is the way to express considerable interest in/concern about the matter.	*A person from a direct culture will think the speaker does not have a strong opinion on the matter.* *A person from an indirect culture will think the speaker is very interested or concerned.*
2. Changing the subject.	The person wants to go on to a new subject.	The person does not want to talk further about the subject now under discussion.	

Technique Used by Speaker	Meaning in a Direct Culture	Meaning in an Indirect Culture	Possible Misinterpretations
3. Saying yes.	Agreement, approval, acceptance, understanding.	Mere acknowledgment that the person heard you; being polite and respectful.	
4. Saying nothing in response to a proposal or suggestion.	The person does not object, disagree with, or have a problem with the proposal/ suggestion.	The person does not approve or does not think it his or her place to comment and would rather say nothing than criticize (especially if the proposal is made in a group setting).	
5. Telling a story that seems to be off the subject.	The person has lost his or her train of thought, has gotten off track, is not very organized.	The person is trying to make a point indirectly, normally a "difficult" point, such as a criticism, refusal, or something disappointing.	
6. Asking a question about or returning to a point previously agreed upon.	The person has forgotten the previous decision or that this point has already been discussed.	The person did not like the previous decision and wants to change it.	

Technique Used by Speaker	Meaning in a Direct Culture	Meaning in an Indirect Culture	Possible Misinterpretations
7. Asking what *you* think in response to your asking for an opinion or making a proposal.	The person wants to know your opinion on the matter.	This usually means no.	
8. Informing a superior about something that is going on.	Asking for some kind of intervention or help.	Being respectful to a superior by keeping him/her informed of routine goings-on.	
9. Qualified answers: Probably, I think so, I'm almost sure, There's a good possibility.	They suggest the likelihood that the thing will happen.	The person is not in agreement with or positive about the matter and doesn't want to say so.	
10. Not mentioning something in a conversation (the significance of what is not said).	Not saying something means you have nothing to say, one way or the other, about that topic.	Not mentioning something can be a way of expressing discomfort about or indicating there is a problem with that topic.	
11. Embedded answer: answering an earlier question in a subsequent part of a conversation.	This technique would not be noticed.	Delicate, embarrassing questions are sometimes answered out of context, where the "answer" can be given obliquely.	

Possible Misinterpretations

Remember in reading the following analyses that in those cases where both the speaker (the person using the technique given in the left-hand column) and the listener are the same type of communicator, then they would normally not be misinterpreting each other.

1. Understatement ("I have one small suggestion.")

   A person from a direct culture will think the speaker does not have a strong opinion on the matter.

   A person from an indirect culture will think the speaker is very interested or concerned.

2. Changing the subject.

   A direct communicator may think the speaker has nothing more to say on the present topic or has lost his or her train of thought. The direct communicator might bring the conversation back to this topic if he or she hasn't finished talking about it, thus upsetting the speaker, who is uncomfortable talking about the subject.

   An indirect communicator may think the speaker is uncomfortable with the topic under discussion and be reluctant to refer to it again.

3. Saying yes.

   A direct communicator will assume the speaker has understood, agreed, approved, accepted whatever is being discussed.

   An indirect communicator will assume that yes is simply a polite acknowledgment and look or probe for the real response from the other person.

4. Saying nothing in response to a proposal or suggestion.

   A direct communicator assumes the speaker will say something if he or she has a problem with or does not agree with or like the proposal; hence, silence means approval.

   An indirect communicator assumes silence means the speaker has some objection to the proposal and will pursue the matter with that person in the appropriate setting.

5. Telling a story that seems to be off the subject.

   A direct communicator will assume the speaker has gone off on a tangent or lost his or her train of thought. The direct person will wait for the speaker to finish and get back to the subject, not paying much attention to the story and perhaps missing an important point that is being made indirectly.

   Since this is not a technique used by direct communicators, there is no chance of misinterpretation here for an indirect communicator. Direct communicators do tell stories on occasion, of course, and when they do, indirect communicators should be careful not to read anything into such stories, for they are usually told for their own sake and not as a way of commenting indirectly on something else.

6. Asking a question about or returning to a point previously agreed upon.

   The direct communicator will think the speaker has forgotten what was said and will simply repeat the gist of the original discussion, when, in fact, the speaker may be trying to reopen the topic in order to get another resolution or decision.

   The indirect communicator will think the speaker wants to reopen the discussion when, in fact, the speaker has simply forgotten the original resolution and wants to be reminded of it or reconfirm it.

7. Asking what *you* think in response to your asking for an opinion or making a proposal.

   A direct communicator will assume the speaker wants to know your own opinion on what you have just proposed or suggested and will give it, thus missing the point, which is that the speaker is not especially taken with the suggestion but doesn't want to come right out and say so.

   An indirect communicator will assume the speaker doesn't think much of the suggestion and may withdraw or amend it when, in fact, the speaker is simply asking for your opinion.

8. Informing a superior about something that is going on.
   Direct communicators may interpret this as a request for a solution or some kind of assistance and offer help where none is needed or wanted by the speaker.

   Indirect communicators might interpret such a conversation as a routine update, a common courtesy toward bosses who like to know everything that's going on—and fail to offer help that was, in fact, being requested by the speaker.

9. Qualified answers: Probably, I think so, I'm almost sure, There's a good possibility.
   Direct communicators interpret these literally as affirmations, when often they are, in fact, polite ways of saying the opposite of what the words mean.

   Indirect communicators hearing these words would take them as polite "nos" when, in fact, they may be meant literally, as near affirmations.

10. Not mentioning something in a conversation (the significance of what is not said).
    Direct communicators would read nothing into the failure of a certain topic to come up, assuming there was nothing to be said about it.

    Indirect communicators might mistakenly read a message into the speaker's failure to bring up a certain topic.

11. Embedded answer: answering an earlier question in a subsequent part of a conversation.
    Direct communicators would normally make no connection between an earlier question and a delayed or buried answer.

    Direct communicators would never use such a technique, so there would be no chance for misinterpretation on the part of an indirect communicator.

Switching Styles

This exercise asks direct communicators (Part 1) and indirect communicators (Part 2) to practice each other's style of expression. You should feel free to try both parts if you wish.

Part 1: For Direct Communicators

In this activity, you are being presented with a series of seven statements which are more characteristic of direct communicators. Read each statement and then try to rephrase it in a manner more sensitive to an indirect style of communication, applying what you have learned in this section of the workbook. It's not necessarily true, by the way, that these seven statements would never be uttered by indirect communicators—they might very well be in certain circumstances—but only that they are less typical.

For the purposes of this activity, imagine the setting to be a meeting in a culture (or with people) where maintaining harmony and saving face are very important. The first item has been done for you.

1. I'm not sure that's such a good idea.
   Do you think that's a good idea?
   Are there any other ideas?
   I like most parts of that idea.

2. That's not exactly the point.

   _____

   _____

   _____

Like many Easterners, Indians don't like to say "no" outright. Sometimes the lack of an answer is tantamount to a "no." In other instances, a "yes" without a follow-up is a "no."
—Manoj Joshi
Passport India

3. I think we should...

_____

_____

_____

4. What do you think, Mr. Cato? (Asking people directly sometimes embarrasses them. How can you find out what Mr. Cato thinks without directly asking him?)

_____

_____

_____

5. Those figures are not completely accurate.

_____

_____

_____

6. That's not the way to do that.

_____

_____

_____

7. I don't agree.

_____

_____

_____

In some of the above cases, even the rephrased statements might still cause embarrassment or loss of face, especially if spoken in front of other people in a meeting. Can you think of any other ways of communicating your message?

1. _____

_____

2. _____

_____

Part 2: For Indirect Communicators

In this activity, you are being presented with a series of seven statements which are more characteristic of indirect communicators. Read each statement and then try to rephrase it in a manner more readily understood by direct communicators, applying what you have learned in this section of the workbook. It's not necessarily true, by the way, that these seven statements would never be uttered by direct communicators—they might very well be in the right circumstances—but only that they are less typical.

For the purposes of this activity, imagine the setting to be a meeting in a culture (or with people) where maintaining harmony and saving face are very important. The first item has been done for you.

1. That is a very interesting viewpoint.
   I don't completely agree.
   We need to talk more about this.
   I see things very differently.

2. This proposal deserves further consideration.

   _____

   _____

   _____

3. Your idea might work.

   _____

   _____

   _____

4. We understand your proposal very well.

   _____

   _____

   _____

5. We will try our best.

   _____

   _____

   _____

6. I heard another story about that project (situation, report, etc.).

_____

_____

_____

7. Can we move on to the next topic?

_____

_____

_____

Suggested Answers

Part 1: For Direct Communicators

1. I'm not sure that's such a good idea.
   Do you think that's a good idea?
   Are there any other ideas?
   I like most parts of that idea.

2. That's not exactly the point.
   That's another good point.
   We could discuss that point later.

3. I think we should...
   What do you think of this idea?
   Has anyone thought about doing it this way?

4. What do you think, Mr. Cato? (Asking people directly sometimes embarrasses them. How can you find out what Mr. Cato thinks without directly asking him?)
   Have we heard all the opinions?
   Are there any other suggestions?
   Does anyone else want to speak?

5. Those figures are not completely accurate.
   I have some other figures here.
   Those figures may be slightly old.

6. That's not the way to do that.
   I would do it this way.
   Have you ever tried doing it this way?
   Has anyone done that a different way?

7. I don't agree.
   That's a good idea, but I have another one.
   What do you think of this idea?
   May I make a small suggestion?

Alternative ways to communicate the messages:

1. Where possible, make your comments to the other person privately, one-on-one, either during a break, after the meeting, or in a brief side conversation.

2. Try to meet with people before a meeting to learn their opinions and make your observations, so you don't have to say these things in public.

Part 2: For Indirect Communicators

1. That is a very interesting viewpoint.
   I don't completely agree.
   We need to talk more about this.
   I see things very differently.

2. This proposal deserves further consideration.
   We don't agree with certain features of this proposal.
   This proposal needs some work.

3. Your idea might work.
   I don't think this idea will work.
   We can come up with a better idea.

4. We understand your proposal very well.
   We have some concerns about your proposal.
   We would like to discuss some changes to your proposal.

5. We will try our best.
   This will be difficult under the circumstances.
   This is not going to be easy.
   I'm not optimistic about this.

6. I heard another story about that project (situation, report, etc.).
   I don't agree with everything you said.
   That's not completely correct.

7. Can we move on to the next topic?
   Let's discuss this later.
   We're not ready to talk about this now.
   We need to get some advice/more information before we can talk about this.

Exercise 3.6

The Body Language Quiz

This is the first of two exercises dealing with the topic of nonverbal communication. The importance of this dimension of communication in a cross-cultural setting will be explained in a moment, but before you read any further, try your hand at the body language quiz.

1. According to psychologist Albert Mehrabian, of the total meaning of a spoken message,

   _____ percent comes from the actual meaning of the words.

   _____ percent comes from the way you say the words (tone, emphasis, etc.).

   _____ percent comes from facial expressions and other non-verbal communication.

2. True or False: A smile is one of the few forms of nonverbal expression that has the same meaning all over the world.

3. The number of different communicative expressions Americans make with their face is
   a. 6
   b. 33
   c. 50
   d. 120

4. Try to guess what percentage of time two negotiators from the following countries maintain eye contact during a typical negotiating session.

   Two Japanese: _____ percent

   Two Americans: _____ percent

   Two Brazilians: _____ percent

All over the world one can make oneself understood by gestures. But in India, impossible. You make a sign that you are in a hurry, that one must be quick; you wave an arm in a manner that the whole world understands—the whole world, but not the Hindu. He does not take it in. He is not even sure it is a gesture.

—Henri Michaux
A Barbarian in Asia

5. True or False: Counting on the fingers, from 1 to 10, is a universal nonverbal gesture.

6. Which groups have the firmest handshakes?

    a. Vietnamese and Filipinos

    b. Germans and Americans

    c. Egyptians and Moroccans

7. In the following cities, try to guess how many times in one hour a typical couple in a cafe touches each other:

    San Juan _____

    Paris _____

    London_____

8. Worldwide, researchers have found approximately how many distinct units of nonverbal communication?

    a. 250

    b. 500

    c. 750

    d. 1,000

Answers

1. _7_ percent comes from the actual meaning of the words.

   _38_ percent comes from the way you say the words (tone, emphasis, etc.).

   _55_ percent comes from facial expressions and other non-verbal communication.

2. False. In Asia a smile can cover up embarrassment or disappointment.

3. b. 33

4. Two Japanese: 13 percent

   Two Americans: 33 percent

   Two Brazilians: 56 percent

5. False. In India, for example, people count the tips of the fingers plus all the joints of the fingers, getting a total of twelve for each hand (the thumb, which does the enumerating, is not counted).

6. b. Germans and Americans

7. San Juan: 180

   Paris: 110

   London: 0

8. d. 1,000

Nonverbal Communication

*Some thirty inches from my
    nose
The frontier of my person goes.*

. . . .

*Stranger, unless with bedroom
    eyes
I beckon you to fraternize
Beware of rudely crossing it;
I have no gun but I can spit.*
            —W. H. Auden
    The Birth of Architecture

The spoken word, as you may have noticed, is not the only means of communication; indeed, in high-context cultures it is often not even the primary means of communication. People in all cultures, whether high- or low-context, rely heavily on various nonverbal behaviors to send messages, the best known of which are probably gestures and facial expressions. As you saw in the body language quiz, the real message in many communication exchanges—or at least a greater *percentage* of the real message—is often conveyed through nonverbal means. Just as culture is a key factor in verbal communication, it also figures prominently in the nonverbal sphere—and plays an identical role: determining the meaning people assign to any given instance of nonverbal behavior.

The reader will remember that behavior does not have inherent meaning, meaning that automatically comes with it, but only the meaning people assign to it. The problem in cross-cultural circumstances is that people from different cultures sometimes assign different meanings to the same behavior. Needless to say, this happens as readily with nonverbal as with verbal communication, so that the message Person A thinks he or she has sent or received may be very different from the message Person B understood or intended.

In the cross-cultural context, nonverbal behaviors can be sorted into three main categories:

1. First are those behaviors which exist in your own culture and in the target culture—and which have the *same* meaning in both. These behaviors don't cause any confusion because sender and receiver assign the same meaning, resulting in successful communication.

2. Next there are those behaviors which exist in both cultures but which have a *different* meaning in each. When one of these behaviors is executed—think of the American okay gesture, a circle made by joining the thumb and the forefinger—you end up sending a different message than you intended (if you're performing the gesture) or misinterpreting the message you receive (if you are the observer).

3. There are also many cases where a particular instance of nonverbal behavior has meaning in the culture of one party in a communication exchange and *no* meaning at all in the culture of the second party. When this happens, there are two possible results:

   - If a particular piece of behavior (think again of a gesture) means something in your culture, and you send this "message" into a culture where it means nothing, the result is that you think you have communicated something when in fact you have not.

   - Or it may happen that in interacting with a person from another culture, either you or that person accidentally executes a behavior that has no meaning in the sender's culture (who doesn't even realize he or she *is* a sender at that moment) but has a very clear meaning in the observer's culture. The result here is that the sender has communicated a message without meaning to and without realizing it.

Needless to say, the second and third categories are the ones which cause confusion in cross-cultural settings. In the exercise which follows, you will see a list of various kinds of nonverbal behaviors (the left-hand column) with two sets of possible interpretations or cultural norms (the next two columns). Because these norms happen to be quite different, when a person from Culture 1 executes that behavior, it may be misinterpreted by an observer from Culture 2, and vice versa. Your task is to read the meaning of the various behaviors in each culture and describe, in the far right column, how each individual is likely to interpret the message coming from the other person. The first one has been done for you as an example.

Nonverbal Chart

Category	Norm for Culture 1	Norm for Culture 2	Possible Misinterpretations
1. Personal space	Greater distance than for Culture 2.	Less distance than Culture 1.	*Culture 1 people may think Culture 2 types stand too close and are a bit aggressive.* *Culture 2 people may think Culture 1 types stand too far away and are reserved, distant, or cold.*
2. Touching	Less frequent than in Culture 2.	More frequent than in Culture 1.	
3. Eye contact	Important to maintain eye contact when listening to someone or when speaking to someone.	Polite to look away and make only fleeting contact, especially with one's elders and superiors.	
4. Holding hands in public	Common for couples in an intimate relationship; rare for same-sex friends.	Common for same-sex friends not in an intimate relationship; very rare for couples.	

Category	Norm for Culture 1	Norm for Culture 2	Possible Misinterpretations
5. Male/female displays of affection in public	Okay to hold hands, lock arms, hug, kiss.	Physical contact very rare in public.	
6. Use of the left hand	No special significance or taboo.	Avoided whenever possible; considered the "dirty" hand.	
7. Loudness of speaking voice	Louder than Culture 2.	Softer than Culture 1.	
8. Shaking hands	Firmer than Culture 2, hand is let go after shaking.	Weaker than Culture 1, hand is sometimes held for a while or taken again and held after shaking.	
9. Pointing the soles of your feet at another person	No particular meaning.	An offensive gesture, a sign of disrespect.	
10. The "yes" gesture with the head	Nodding the head up and down. The "no" gesture is shaking the head from side to side.	Rolling the head from side to side.	

Possible Misinterpretations

1. Personal space.

   Culture 1 people may think Culture 2 types stand too close and are a bit aggressive.

   Culture 2 people may think Culture 1 types stand too far away and are reserved, distant, or cold.

2. Touching.

   People from Culture 1 may think people from Culture 2 touch too much and are a bit rough or pushy.

   People from Culture 2 may think people from Culture 1 don't touch enough and are cold, unfriendly, and distant.

3. Eye contact.

   People from Culture 1 may think people from Culture 2 are not paying attention or cannot be trusted.

   People from Culture 2 may think people from Culture 1 are rude and aggressive (by not showing proper respect in looking down). Note: if this nonverbal misinterpretation is teamed up with the first two, a pattern starts to emerge that makes each speaker look progressively worse to the other.

4. Holding hands in public.

   People from Culture 1 may think couples in Culture 2 are quite reserved. On the other hand, they may be shocked to see same-sex friends holding hands and may mistakenly think they are romantically involved.

   People from Culture 2 may think couples in Culture 1 have no modesty or shame and may think that same-sex friends are quite cold and reserved because they don't hold hands.

5. Male/female displays of affection in public.

   People in Culture 1 may think couples in Culture 2 are repressed or at least not very warm and affectionate.

   People in Culture 2 may think couples in Culture 1 have no modesty or shame.

6. Use of the left hand.

   This has no particular meaning in Culture 1, so these people will not see this "behavior" when it is performed by people in Culture 2.

People in Culture 2 may be insulted when people in Culture 1, in all innocence, use the left hand to pass them things, take things from them, and so on. If someone in Culture 2 deliberately tries to offend someone in Culture 1 by using this gesture, the message will not be received by the person in Culture 1.

7. Loudness of speaking voice.

People in Culture 1 may think people in Culture 2 speak too softly and may also not notice when someone in Culture 2 has raised his or her voice in anger or frustration, for example, because the raised voice is the level at which Culture 1 people normally speak.

People in Culture 2 may think people in Culture 1 are agitated or upset because they speak in louder voices, the voice Culture 2 people only use when they are angry or agitated.

8. Shaking hands.

Culture 1 people may interpret the weaker handshake of Culture 2 people to mean that a person is not very self-confident or strong. If a Culture 2 person takes or continues to hold a Culture 1 person's hand during the ensuing conversation, the Culture 1 person will find this degree of touching very strange.

Culture 2 people may find the firm handshake of a Culture 1 person to be quite rough and aggressive. Furthermore, if Culture 1 people do not hold on to or take the hand of Culture 2 people during the ensuing conversation or remove their hand if a Culture 2 person takes it, Culture 2 people may think Culture 1 people are cold and unfriendly.

9. Pointing the soles of your feet at another person.

As this has no meaning in Culture 1, these people will not see this as "behavior" if it is performed by people in Culture 2.

People in Culture 2 may be offended if someone from Culture 1, in all innocence, points his or her feet at them. If someone in Culture 2 deliberately tries to offend someone in Culture 1 by using this gesture, the message will not be received by the person in Culture 1.

10. The "yes" gesture with the head.

    To people in Culture 1, the "yes" gesture from Culture 2 can easily be mistaken for the "no" gesture of Culture 1.

    To people in Culture 2, the "no" gesture from Culture 1 can be mistaken for the "yes" gesture of Culture 2.

Dialogues Revisited

Now that you have completed this chapter, reread the dialogues in the diagnostic exercise (exercise 3.1) on pages 89-90 to see whether you notice anything new in light of what you have learned about communication styles in the foregoing exercises. Then read the analyses below for a description of the cultural differences that were being illustrated in the dialogues. (It's possible you will have seen differences other than those described below.)

1. A Call from Hari

If you are a low-context, direct communicator, as Bob apparently is, chances are this dialogue was virtually impenetrable. Why? Because direct communicators use language to convey meaning, and in this dialogue, the man known as Hari has conveyed meaning not in words at all but in a typical high-context manner—by not doing something he regularly does. Indeed, this is called manipulating the context and would be immediately understood by another high-context communicator, as it is by Magda.

To be more specific, Hari apparently has a weekly meeting with Magda at her workplace. But now, in a departure from the norm, Hari is not coming. And the point is that in some cultures, those we have called high-context, a departure from the norm is a classic way of sending a message, usually that all is not well. That is precisely why Magda is in such a hurry to get over to Hari's office and see what's wrong.

Bob has missed this entirely, taking Hari at his word ("He said he was sorry and he would try to come next week") and not even noticing the departure from the norm. Or maybe he did notice it, but being a low-context communicator, he did not realize it contained another message. (It's possible, by the way, that Hari should be taken at his word, that he is in fact too busy to come this week and there is no other message here at all. The point is that in high-context cultures, where people use several channels for sending messages, you can't be as sure about that as you can in low-context cultures, where you're usually safe taking what people say at face value.)

2. A Bit of a Nuisance

This dialogue illustrates how two common techniques of communication, understatement and changing the subject, are interpreted differently by direct and indirect communicators. Karl and Gitti are two direct communicators reviewing a conversation Karl had with a third person, the somewhat more indirect Arabella. As is their norm, Karl and Gitti have interpreted Arabella's phrase "a bit of a nuisance" literally, assuming she means just that and nothing more. Indirect communicators, however, will often use understatement like this to suggest a much stronger feeling which, for any number of reasons, they do not want to express openly. Hence, "a bit of a nuisance" should be examined more closely to see if it means what it seems to on the surface or if it's standing in for something stronger, for what Arabella is not comfortable saying.

Any doubt about what the phrase might mean is erased when Arabella then changes the subject. Although this is interpreted as a good sign by Karl and Gitti (that Arabella is moving on to another topic), they have probably misinterpreted this behavior. For Arabella and many indirect communicators, changing the subject is often used as a way of indicating that they find the present subject uncomfortable to talk about and want to get away from it, and not, as the two speakers assume, that they have nothing more to say about the present subject.

3. Saturday Shift

Communication in this dialogue goes astray from the very first line in which Ms. Jones, from a direct culture, thinks she has just told Mr. Wu about a need she has for workers on Saturday. In point of fact, however, Mr. Wu, from an indirect culture, has not heard this first line as a statement of a need but as an indirect, veiled, and very polite request to come in on Saturday, for this is, in fact, almost exactly how Mr. Wu would make such a request in his culture.

Things go rapidly downhill from here. Wu answers this "request" in the negative ("I see," which in his culture is a polite way of saying no without actually using the word). In his culture, if Wu could come in on Saturday, he would immediately say so at this point; that he does not, that the best he can manage is "I see," is a clear indication that he can't come in.

This is not exactly how Ms. Jones reads it. Indeed, Ms. Jones doesn't even realize she's asked a question yet, much less that it has already been answered. Accordingly, she now proceeds to ask Wu if he can come in. Wu is taken aback, of course, having already said he can't, but he reiterates his position with another indirect negative: "Yes, I think so." Needless to say, this is probably going to come across as a yes to the hapless Ms. Jones, who interprets things quite literally.

Imagine Wu's surprise at the next line, "That'll be a great help." He has twice told Ms. Jones he can't come in, and she still thinks he can. Now Wu doesn't know what to do, so he tries what for him must be called the direct approach, telling Ms. Jones exactly why he won't be there on Saturday—it is his son's birthday. Ms. Jones, who has been in the dark for most of this conversation (from Wu's point of view, that is) goes even further astray at this point, finding Wu's comment on the birthday quite far from the subject under discussion.

Saturday isn't going to be a good day for Ms. Jones, nor is Monday shaping up to be much fun for Mr. Wu.

4. Rewrite

This dialogue goes by so fast it's hard to believe culture had a chance to get a word in edgewise, but it did, twice in fact. The more direct Susan is used to getting honest feedback; if people like something, they will say so, and if they don't like it, they will also say so—and no one's feelings get hurt. We're all grownups here, after all.

But Yang clearly isn't used to being quite so blunt. His way of giving feedback, negative feedback in this case, is to toss the question back to the questioner—"Generally tighter than the first draft, don't you think?"—rather than have to say he doesn't much like the rewrite. Beyond that Yang also gives two other subtle suggestions of how he feels: he gives rather weak praise (about how "tight" the rewrite is, out of all the things he could have said at this point) and he leaves the decision to send the piece down for printing up to Susan when he could easily have said yes or no. Whenever you find a yes/no question tossed back at you, there's a good chance (at least in indirect cultures) that the other person doesn't want to answer the question. And when someone is afraid of answering a question, it's usually because he or she wants to avoid saying no and disappointing you. After all, if the answer is yes, meaning you'll be pleased, why would anyone be afraid to say so?

Most of this is lost on Susan, who is not used to these indirect techniques and instead relies on people's words to convey what they are thinking. When someone praises something, then it means they like it, not that they really don't like it and have found this innocuous feature to praise as a way of saying the rest is junk. And when someone says something is up to you, they mean it's your decision, not that they're not happy and just don't want to say so. If they're not happy, so goes the thinking of direct communicators, people will use words to the effect of "By the way, I'm not happy."

Culture in the Workplace

Culture inhabits all behaviors, whether you're at home interacting with friends and family, or at work interacting with coworkers, bosses, and subordinates. While there are no doubt some workplace norms that transcend culture and are common to everyone, no two cultures think about or carry out workplace activities in exactly the same way.

In this section of the workbook, you will be looking at the dimensions of culture that have particular significance for the workplace, including the manager/subordinate relationship, attitudes toward uncertainty and toward work, the key to productivity, and the source of status. This is not to suggest that the topics covered under the other chapters, such as building blocks (chapter 2) or styles of communication (chapter 3), don't also apply to the workplace, for they do indeed, but only that the topics covered here relate more specifically to how people conceive of and carry out their work.

The [folks] of my own
  stock
They may do ill or well
But they tell the lies I am
  wonted to,
And they are used to the
  lies I tell;
And we do not need
  interpreters
When we go to buy and
  sell.
  —Rudyard Kipling
  "The Stranger"

Dialogues

For a Spaniard, success lies in the title as much as in the salary, and much more than in the work.

—Helen Wattley Ames
Spain Is Different

You will begin your consideration of workplace cultural issues in the same way you did in chapters 2 and 3—by trying to figure out the following four dialogues. As always, the task here is to read these brief conversations, each of which illustrates a cultural difference between the two speakers, and try to identify what that difference is.

Once again, the differences won't necessarily jump out at you, but they are there if you can find them. If you can't find them, don't despair; the information in the rest of this chapter will enable you to get to the bottom of the dialogues. After you have worked on the dialogues, you should go on and complete the other exercises. Later, you will be asked to return to this exercise and reread it in light of what you will then know about culture in the workplace.

1. Database

ALEXEI: Did you hear? We won't be getting a new staff person after all.

MARTHA: I know. We'll never get our database caught up.

ALEXEI: Well, we can resubmit the request next fiscal year.

MARTHA: Actually, I've got a better idea. I've heard about some new software that makes adding to a database much easier than the system we're using.

ALEXEI: Has it been tried in organizations like ours?

MARTHA: I'm not sure, but I've heard they give it free to nonprofits like us.

ALEXEI: We'd have to train everyone in it.

MARTHA: For sure.

2. Rough Edges

DEBBIE: I'd like you to work with Peter on this project.

MIKO: Yes, ma'am.

DEBBIE: Is something wrong?

MIKO: Excuse me, ma'am, but I don't work very well with Peter. It's my fault, I'm sure.

DEBBIE: No it isn't. I know about Peter. But don't let him get to you. Sure, he's a little rough around the edges, but he really knows programming. And that's what counts.

MIKO: Yes, ma'am.

3. One Less Headache

AMANDA: I think we'll have to hire two part-time workers to get through this period.

HASSAN: I don't see any other way.

AMANDA: I'll call personnel tomorrow to get the paperwork started.

HASSAN: Did you speak to Ali?

AMANDA: The chief? He's in meetings all day. Besides, it's my division, and I've got hiring authority.

HASSAN: Yes. I'm sure he'll approve.

AMANDA: Well, that's one less headache.

4. Dr. de Leon

JULIE: I heard the board has chosen a new CEO.

CARLOS: Yes, they've appointed Dr. Manuel Cabeza de Leon of the de Leon family.

JULIE: Who is he?

CARLOS: It's an old family with large landholdings in Guadalajara province.

JULIE: But what's his background?

CARLOS: I just told you.

JULIE: I mean has he worked in textiles before? Does he have any experience in the business?

CARLOS: I don't know.

JULIE: You don't know? Do you think he's a good choice?

CARLOS: Dr. de Leon? I'm sure.

Exercise 4.2

Power Distance

The hierarchical nature of Indian society demands that there is a boss and that the boss should be seen to be the boss. Everyone else just does as they are told, and even if they know the boss is 100% wrong, no one will argue.

—Gitanjali Kolanad
Culture Shock: India

One of the most important and frequently troublesome work-related cultural differences involves the phenomenon known as power distance.[1] The significance of power distance actually extends well beyond the workplace, having as its focus the attitude of a society toward inequality—how cultures deal with distinctions between people in their access to power and their level of status—but it manifests especially strongly in workplace relations. In its most conspicuous manifestation, it determines the proper role of managers and subordinates and the nature of their interactions.

Brief descriptions of the two poles of this concept, *high* and *low power distance*, are given below.

> *High Power Distance*: These cultures accept that inequalities in power and status are natural or existential. People accept that some among them will have more power and influence than others in the same way they accept that some people are taller than others. Those with power tend to emphasize it, to hold it close and not delegate or share it, and to distinguish themselves as much as possible from those who do not have power. They are, however, expected to accept the responsibilities that go with power, especially that of looking after those beneath them. Subordinates are not expected to take initiative and are closely supervised.

---

[1] The exercises on power distance and uncertainty in this chapter build upon the groundbreaking work of Geert Hofstede. See Recommended Reading.

Low Power Distance: People in these cultures see inequalities in power and status as man-made and largely artificial; it is not natural, though it may be convenient, that some people have power over others. Those with power, therefore, tend to deemphasize it, to minimize the differences between themselves and subordinates, and to delegate and share power to the extent possible. Subordinates are rewarded for taking initiative and do not like close supervision.

No culture, of course, will be exclusively high or low in power distance—all cultures will have elements of both poles—but cultures do tend to be *more* one than the other. As always, individuals in any given culture, because of personal differences, can be anywhere along the continuum, and may very well be at one spot in one set of circumstances and somewhere else in another set. On the whole, however, you should expect to find most individuals on the same side of the dichotomy as their culture in general.

The exercise which follows asks you to take the definitions of *high* and *low power distance* presented above and apply them to specific examples of behavior. Below you will find a list of thirteen items, each of which is more representative of one pole of this dimension than the other. Read each item and put an *H* next to those behaviors more consistent with high power distance and an *L* next to those more consistent with low.

_____ 1.   People are less likely to question the boss; students don't question teachers.

_____ 2.   Expressing your ideas openly could get you into trouble.

_____ 3.   Expressing your ideas openly is encouraged.

_____ 4.   The chain of command is mainly for convenience.

_____ 5.   Workers prefer precise instructions from superiors.

_____ 6.   Subordinates and bosses are interdependent.

_____ 7.   Bosses are independent; subordinates are dependent.

_____ 8. Elitism is more common and more easily tolerated; those in power have special privileges.

_____ 9. The chain of command is sacrosanct.

_____ 10. Authoritarian and paternalistic management style is more common.

_____ 11. Consultative and democratic management style is more common.

_____ 12. Interaction between boss and subordinate is formal.

_____ 13. Interaction between boss and subordinate is more informal.

Suggested Answers

_H_ 1. Superiors are shown more deference in high power distance cultures.

_H_ 2. It's better to see what superiors are thinking.

_L_ 3. Superiors are not threatened by differences of opinion.

_L_ 4. In high power distance cultures, the chain of command should be strictly observed.

_H_ 5. Workers don't want to make mistakes and get criticized for doing so.

_L_ 6. Bosses are independent of workers in high power distance cultures.

_H_ 7. Rank has its privileges.

_H_ 8. It's accepted that the higher up you go, the more privileges you will have (to go along with the increased responsibility).

_H_ 9. Skipping people in the chain of command can be seen as trying to usurp their power.

_H_ 10. Managers flex their management muscles.

_L_ 11. A manager is just one of the team.

_H_ 12. The distance between managers and subordinates is emphasized.

_L_ 13. We're all in this together.

Exercise 4.3

Comparing Workplace Norms across Cultures

Few Germans would sell their umbrella in the desert; it just might rain.

—Philip Glouchevitch
Juggernaut Hill

In this final continuum exercise, you will be comparing the workplace norms of your own culture with those of the target cultures you are interested in. Once you see your culture's view of various workplace issues and the view of your target cultures, you will have identified major cultural differences that are a likely source of and explanation for common misunderstandings and misinterpretations.

Once again, you will use the continuum technique to make these comparisons. You will find five continua, with the poles or extremes of each topic described at either end. For each continuum, read the two descriptions and put a vertical line somewhere along the continuum, depending on which explanation you think more accurately describes the view of people in your culture in general on this issue. Not everyone will take the same view, of course, but try nevertheless to make a generalization about the "typical" or average person from your culture.

For example, on the continuum marked Power Distance, if you think the description under Low (left side) more accurately describes your culture's position on this issue, you will put your mark nearer to the left. For purposes of marking, remember to think of each continuum as being divided into five segments, starting at the left:

extreme left	Put your mark here if the text at the left describes your culture very accurately.
halfway to the middle	Put your mark here if the text at the left is more or less accurate about your culture.
in the middle	Put your mark here if your culture is a true combination of the text at the right and left.

| halfway from the middle | Put your mark here if the text on the right is more or less accurate about your culture. |
| extreme right | Put your mark here if the text at the right describes your culture very accurately. |

The first continuum presents the concept of power distance, already introduced and examined earlier in this chapter. The other four, however, deal with concepts you have not yet encountered: attitude toward uncertainty, attitude toward work, key to productivity, and source of status. While certain of these concepts have implications outside one's work and job, all four are especially significant for understanding norms and expectations in the workplace.

The essence of each of these concepts should be clear from the explanations given on the chart, but a brief word here about each might also be helpful:

Attitude toward uncertainty *refers to how a culture feels about change and tradition and about what is new and different. It also examines cultural attitudes toward taking risks and failing.*

Attitude toward work *examines what motivates people to work, what they want to get out of their work, and the proper relationship between the demands of work and one's personal life.*

Key to productivity *looks at what behaviors are valued and rewarded in the workplace and the relationship between employer and employee.*

Source of status *refers to how people come by their status, rank, and position—in society in general and in their organizations.*

After you have marked all five continua, you can then use the chart to compare your own culture with your target culture (or cultures) and identify important differences. You can do this in one of two ways:

1. You can give the chart to someone from the target culture and ask that person to complete it the same way you did, following the instructions given above.
2. You can consult the master list on pages 140-41. This list locates a number of cultures or cultural groupings on the chart.

What do these marks mean? While these are all generalizations and therefore not predictive of what individuals in any given culture might think, each mark represents how the people in that culture in general feel about that item on the continuum. More precisely, the marks indicate

- what the people in that culture think of as natural, normal, right, and good;
- how these people assume everyone feels about these issues; and
- which perspective these people use to interpret and judge the behavior of others (including you).

Where there is a wide gap between your mark and that of someone from the target culture, you can assume that you and that person may not see eye to eye on this matter. He or she may think your behavior or attitude is strange or surprising, and you may think the same about that person. And each of you is likely to misinterpret or misunderstand the actions of the other in certain situations.

This doesn't mean that you and that other person will never understand each other or be able to work together successfully, but it does mean that you may have very little intuitive understanding of the other person with regard to this particular item, and vice versa. In other words, each of you will have to make some effort and exercise patience in trying to understand the other.

Finally, remember that context determines everything in human interaction. Nothing happens "in general"; things only happen in context, in specific circumstances. And depending on those circumstances, another person's position on power distance or source of status, for example, may or may not play a role, or at least not a deciding role, in a particular interaction. But these cultural characteristics are always there as a potential, waiting for an opportunity to show themselves.

Power Distance

|—————————|—————————|—————————|—————————|

Low   **High**

Democratic management style; power is not usually jealously guarded, manager shares authority with subordinates; subordinates take initiative and are not overly deferential to managers; subordinates do not like to be micromanaged; decision making tends to be consultative; okay to say no/disagree with the boss; manager/subordinate relations are fairly informal; rank has few privileges.

Authoritarian; power is centralized; one defers to authority; managers hold on to power, not much delegation of authority; subordinates do not take initiative but wait for explicit instructions; decisions are made at the top; one does not openly disagree with/say no to the boss; rank has its privileges; manager/subordinate relations are formal.

Attitude toward Uncertainty

|—————————|—————————|—————————|—————————|

Positive   **Skeptical**

People are not afraid of taking risks or of failing; trial and error/experimenting is how we learn and improve our products and services; what is different is interesting; change is positive; new is often better; tradition is not valued for its own sake; the "way we have always done things" is not necessarily the best way; what we don't know can't hurt us.

Taking risks and failing have strong negative consequences and should be avoided if at all possible; one doesn't try something until one knows it will work; what is different can be dangerous; change is threatening; new is not necessarily better; traditions should be respected and are a good guide to the future; there's a good reason for "the way we have always done things"; what we don't know can be troubling.

Attitude toward Work

|—————————|—————————|—————————|—————————|

Achievement

People are motivated by achievement; ambition is rewarded; being successful means moving up, getting ahead, and having greater power and responsibility; professional opportunity/the chance to make more money is more important than job security; if people have to choose between work and family, they may choose work; one lives to work.

Quality of Life

A better quality of life is what motivates people to work; a pleasant work setting and good relations with coworkers are as motivating as the chance to make more money and move up; having time to spend with family/friends is as important as the lure of achievement; more power and responsibility are not automatically attractive; success means you are admired and respected by others; one works to live.

Key to Productivity

|—————————|—————————|—————————|—————————|

Results

Focusing on the task ensures success; what matters most in employees is their productivity and output, which are related to technical skills and experience; conflict is sometimes necessary to clear the air and move forward; getting results is ultimately more important than how you get them; employee/employer relationship is often opportunistic; employee loyalty is not as important as performance/productivity.

Harmony

Harmony in the workplace ensures the success of an organization; what matters in employees is their ability to get along/work well with others, which is related to personal qualities (more than technical skills); conflict should be minimized because of disruptive consequences; how you get results is as important as the results themselves; employer/employee relationship is like a family; loyalty is expected and reciprocal.

Source of Status

Achieved

Meritocracy; rank, status, and respect must be earned and do not come with the position or title; family name and social class do not confer automatic status; people are respected and promoted based on their performance and achievements, regardless of age or seniority; age/seniority do not guarantee respect or status; it is relatively easy to change your status (to move up); people of higher rank/status should not act superior to/better than those of lesser.

Ascribed

Autocracy; rank, position, and title confer automatic status and respect; social class/family name confer initial status (but it can be lost if you do not perform well); achievements are important for promotion, but age and seniority are also highly valued; age and seniority confer automatic status and respect; it is difficult to change your status (especially to move up); people should be careful not to behave above/below their station in life.

Position of Selected Cultures

A number of cultures or cultural groupings have been selected for inclusion on this chart. The positions given here reflect either where nationals of these countries/regions have consistently placed themselves on this chart in numerous workshops and training seminars given by the author or where the author has placed these cultures after consulting various surveys and studies in the literature of the intercultural field. Remember that these placements are approximations and that they indicate the position of a culture as a whole on these matters, not of individuals. Even then, it's possible the reader may not agree with where his or her culture has been placed or even where other cultures have been placed. The best way to use these continuum charts is not to take our word for any of this but to hand them to a person from another culture and let that individual speak for his or her own society. If any of your target cultures do not appear on this chart, you may be able to infer their position by noting the placement of a similar culture.

Power Distance

```
  UK    US                        J      F      A    ME,C        R
  G                                S                  M,I   SEA
  |------------|-----------------|-----------------|-------------|
Low                                                             High
```

Attitude toward Uncertainty

```
  US                   SEA    I      A     ME     R    F,S    J
          UK                  G      C                  M
  |------------|-----------------|-----------------|-------------|
Positive                                                   Skeptical
```

Attitude toward Work

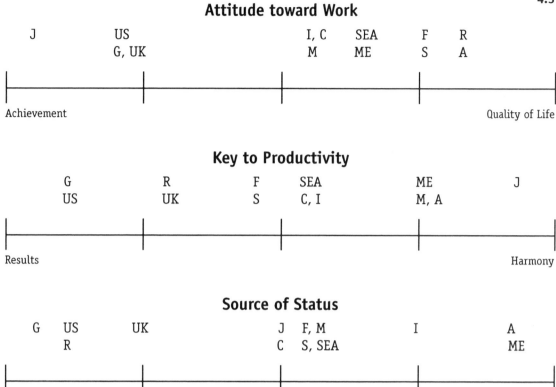

```
J          US                        I, C    SEA      F       R
           G, UK                     M       ME       S       A
```

Achievement   Quality of Life

Key to Productivity

```
      G           R          F      SEA           ME           J
      US          UK         S      C, I          M, A
```

Results   Harmony

Source of Status

```
   G   US      UK                 J    F, M        I            A
       R                          C    S, SEA                   ME
```

Achieved   Ascribed

A—Africa C—China F—France G—Germany I—India J—Japan
M—Mexico ME—Middle East R—Russia S—Spain
SEA—Southeast Asia UK—United Kingdom US—United States

Exercise 4.4

What Would You Do?

Not only can't you change careers so easily in Europe, most people don't even think of it. Mainly the European becomes tired at the very idea of risk.
—Stuart Miller
Understanding Europeans

The following four incidents describe workplace conflicts which occurred because of a cultural difference. Your task is to read each one and, using what you have learned about culture in this and the preceding chapters, indicate in the space below the incident what you would do or say if you were faced with this situation.

1. Offshore Partner

You are a team leader in the technical support division of a large manufacturing company in a low power distance culture. Your company is famous for its informal and flat organizational culture: there are few layers of management and your engineers work for the most part on their own, only coming to you when they have a problem or a question. Your company has recently entered into an agreement with an offshore partner (in a high power distance culture) to provide you with software programmers for one of your important projects. These programmers will be with you for an eighteen-month period, and now, after the arrival of the first group, there are some problems.

The programmers do not seem willing or able to work without very close supervision and, in fact, seem unwilling to take responsibility for their work. They expect you to make even the most routine decisions, and they always check with you before undertaking even moderately important tasks. In dealing with internal clients (divisions that you and these foreign programmers are developing software for), they always defer to you and do not give these clients answers to their questions or responses to their requests on the spot, although it is well within their job description to do so. All this means you're having to spend a lot more time with these people than you should, so much that you have almost no time for your other employees. What should you do?

_____

_____

_____

2. Trial and Error

You have been posted overseas with a nonprofit foreign aid organization. Your area of expertise is environmental cleanup, and the country in which you work is trying to recover from decades of abusing its natural resources, especially water. You are in charge of setting up a demonstration water-filtering plant in a certain district, but you are encountering strong resistance from the district supervisor. He wants to know if this technique has been tried anywhere else in his country, and when you say no, he asks why he should let you "experiment at [his] expense."

You point out that it's very important to see if this technique will work in his country. If it doesn't, then how much better it will be to know that now before going ahead and installing these plants in every district. He will be a hero for sponsoring this trial.

He says he will lose his job if this high-profile experiment fails and asks you why you can't know ahead of time if the plant is going to work. If you're not sure it's going to work, then you should spend more time perfecting the technology. "When the technology is perfect, then you can try it out in my district," he says. What do you do?

_____

_____

_____

3. Peer Teaching

You are an expatriate adviser working in an AIDS education program in a developing country. Your sponsoring organization has designed a peer teaching project that involves training high school seniors in basic AIDS prevention techniques, which they then teach to younger teenagers in special after-school workshops. Research in your own culture has shown that when teens get this particular message from other, older teens, they pay much more attention than when an adult lectures them on this topic.

Your organization has conducted a number of training sessions around the country for the seniors, a cadre of whom have already begun to hold the after-school workshops. At a meeting with an official from the Ministry of Health today, you heard that there have been numerous complaints about these workshops from teachers around the country. The teachers maintain that to have high school seniors holding classes undermines the teachers' respect and credibility. Apparently, there have already been discipline problems in some schools. "We put teachers on a pedestal in our culture," this official explained to you, "because of the high regard we hold for knowledge and a sound education. To have students teaching other students makes our teachers look bad." Now what?

---

4. Know-How

You are an expatriate from a low power distance culture living in a high power distance country. You were about to return to your home culture when a large corporation in the overseas country hired you. They were looking in particular for the kind of marketing expertise your company is famous for. Now that you have been on board for a few months, you're not having a good time. Although these people say they hired you for your marketing know-how, whenever you try to make suggestions or changes in the way your new company does business, you meet with resistance.

Today your boss has had an unusually frank discussion with you, laying out the reasons for the trouble you're having. He says your problem is that you are too outspoken and don't know your place. You disagree with your superiors in front of others and sometimes correct them in front of others when they say something wrong. You also make too many decisions without checking with other people, even though, as your boss admits, you know more about the subject than those people do.

Now you're confused. You thought you'd been hired for what you know, but whenever you try to put what you know into practice, your supervisors seem offended. What do you do now?

_____

_____

_____

Discussion

1. Offshore Partner

You obviously need to encourage your expat programmers to work more independently. The problem is that they are now in a low power distance culture, but they are continuing to behave the way they would if they were back home. They aren't trying to upset you; they simply assume that you expect and appreciate this kind of behavior. In other words, you and they have the same goal: that these expatriates will be effective and successful in their assignments. What they don't realize is that the *way* one is effective and successful in your culture is very different from the way one is in theirs.

Seen in this light, your task here becomes easier. You need to explain to your expatriate programmers that while you understand what lies behind their behavior (that it is well intentioned), it is unexpected and counterproductive in your culture. Explain that managers here actually do want employees to work independently, with a minimum of supervision, and to make decisions on their own (if it's part of their job). Assure them that mistakes are more readily understood and forgiven in this environment than in their home culture, especially with new employees. Point out that managers in your culture don't expect much deference to authority figures and fully expect subordinates to use any authority that is delegated to them.

Once these norms are made explicit to your expats, once they understand what behaviors and attitudes are necessary to succeed in your culture and company, they will most likely try to change their counterproductive behaviors. One word of warning, however: don't assume that once you communicate your expectations, your expats will be able to change all their behaviors overnight. It takes a little longer than that to change years of habit, but they will come around if you give them time, especially if their efforts to do so are rewarded.

2. Trial and Error

The central cultural issue here involves the attitude toward change and taking risks. In high uncertainty avoidance cultures where change is viewed with suspicion, where it is avoided if at all possible, then trying something new is by definition a non-starter.

Your approach here should be two-pronged: convince this man that the risks of what you want to do are minimal and that the possible rewards are considerable. He needs reassurance. If it's feasible, you should try to implement your project in bite-sized chunks, small increments which minimize the consequences and visibility of failure. A big risk may be more than he can handle, so give him a series of small risks.

You might try to get more data from other places where this scheme has been tried or bring in people the supervisor respects and will listen to and have them defend the project. The best approach is to get people above him to support the project and identify themselves with it; this gives him protection in the event that things go wrong.

Whatever you do, you will have to proceed much more slowly and cautiously in this culture than in your own. You will probably want to add several months to your projected completion date.

3. Peer Teaching

There is probably no reason why peer teaching can't work in this society, though you might want to reexamine your data showing that messages received from peers are more likely to take hold. If this is a culture where status is ascribed, where teachers teach and students listen, then blurring the status distinctions isn't going to win you any friends. In any case, your best chance here is to involve the teachers much more in the program and at the same time redefine the role of the peers. You may want to have teachers leading the workshops, with the seniors participating in a more subordinate role. The seniors can still give the exact same input but in a show that is clearly run by teachers. Or you may want to try some variation on this theme.

The main point is that students should not be crowded onto the same pedestal heretofore reserved for teachers. Any redesign of the project that makes it clear that seniors and teachers are not equals should at least lower the volume of the criticism. Strictly speaking, this would no longer be peer teaching, but it would still accomplish the goal of peers telling other peers about safe sex.

4. Know-How

Your low power distance behaviors are getting in the way of your effectiveness here. The problem isn't that people don't value and need your technical expertise; that's why they hired you. The problem is in the way you're delivering your expertise. Being a technical expert doesn't excuse you from the necessity of observing cultural norms, and apparently one of the norms in this culture is that you defer to authority figures. And this deference extends even to situations where they say things that are incorrect or offer suggestions that make no sense.

It's not that you say nothing at such times or that you're not supposed to bring your expertise to bear in these situations; it's all in how you give your input. To begin with, you can take your colleagues aside and get your message across privately, which will allow them to save face and retain the respect of their subordinates. Or, if you feel you must say something in a meeting, phrase it as delicately as possible, drawing attention to anything your colleagues said that was right and making only a passing reference to what was incorrect or ill advised. Don't worry that you are being too vague; in cultures such as this, people readily understand indirect, oblique references.

As for your decision-making style, once again the problem isn't that you shouldn't be making these decisions but that you shouldn't make them without consulting your superiors. While it's quite true your superiors may not have anything substantive to contribute, it's common courtesy in high power distance cultures to keep senior management informed at all times and also to ask permission to decide what you have already decided.

In many cultures style is just as important as substance. At the end of the day in such cultures, the expert with the right style prevails as often as the expert with the right answers.

Dialogues Revisited

Now that you have completed this chapter, reread the dialogues in the diagnostic exercise (exercise 4.1) on pages 128-29 to see whether you have any new insights in light of what you have learned about workplace cultural norms in the foregoing exercises. Then read the analyses below for descriptions of the cultural differences that were being illustrated in the dialogues. (It's possible you will have seen differences other than those described below.)

1. Database

This dialogue illustrates certain key differences between high and low uncertainty avoidance cultures. Both Martha and Alexei want to find a solution to the staffing problem that has just resurfaced in their office, but their approaches are notably different. Martha favors trial and error, experimenting with the new software to see if it might work and, if it doesn't, then trying something else. She's not afraid of taking risks or of failing. She sees failing as part of problem solving, the price you sometimes have to pay to learn what you need to learn, but not as a problem in and of itself. Failing is a means to success, not the opposite of success.

Alexei has a different view of failing; it's not necessarily a way station on the road to succeeding but the proverbial end of the line. It's important, therefore, to avoid failure if at all possible—and if it's not possible, then to think twice before even risking it. Alexei only wants to try things he knows will work ("Has it been tried in organizations like ours?"), not to try things to see *if* they will work.

These two also differ in their attitude toward change. For Martha, change is natural and inevitable, something you simply handle when it comes up. For Alexei, change is much more daunting; you first decide *if* you can handle it before you allow it to come up. Change shouldn't be undertaken lightly, and in many cases it shouldn't be undertaken at all.

2. Rough Edges

What constitutes the ideal worker varies from culture to culture. For Debbie, technical expertise, the actual skills needed to do the job, are high on the list of desirable attributes. But for Miko, what seems to be equally important is the ability to get along with coworkers. Peter's rough edges might be overlooked in Debbie's culture because he can get the job done, but in cultures where the *way* you get the job done is as important as completing the task, his lack of interpersonal skills would be a serious drawback. Imagine, for example, those cultures which value harmony, the saving of face, and teams which work well together; how would Peter's apparent abrasiveness be regarded there?

This doesn't mean, by the way, that more individualist cultures would not also be put off by Peter, only that they might draw the line in a different place. High achievers, which Peter seems to be, are given more latitude in some cultures than others. Also, this does not mean that collectivist cultures don't care about an employee's technical abilities, but they might place relatively more emphasis on interpersonal skills.

3. One Less Headache

This dialogue touches on the concept of power distance. In Amanda's low power distance culture, managers don't normally want or expect to be consulted on routine decisions, especially decisions subordinates have been given the authority to make on their own. Managers in these cultures would particularly not appreciate being consulted on such decisions when they're busy with more important matters. Managers in low power distance cultures delegate authority and fully expect subordinates to use that authority without checking in with them.

Apparently this isn't how it works in Hassan's high power distance culture. When he says he's sure Ali will approve the hiring of part-time workers, Hassan doesn't mean, as Amanda thinks he does, that there is therefore no need to run this plan by Ali; he is saying, rather, that Ali will of course say yes when Hassan asks for permission. Which he had better do, for in these cultures managers may technically delegate authority, but they very much appreciate and expect the courtesy of being asked for permission to use that authority. Subordinates routinely check in with management in such cultures, even if it's only a formality; indeed, formality is one of the cornerstones of the manager/subordinate relationship in high power distance cultures.

As the dialogue ends, Amanda has misread Hassan, who has in fact just advised her to check with Ali. Amanda isn't planning to, naturally, and probably fancies that Ali will thank her for not having bothered him with such a minor matter. Stay tuned.

4. Dr. de Leon

This dialogue compares cultures where status must be achieved to those where status is ascribed. In the former, status is earned through one's accomplishments, the things you have done. When someone reaches a position of prominence and responsibility, it is because that person has worked hard for the status that has been conferred upon him or her. Or so Julie believes, which is why she keeps pressing Carlos for evidence of how Dr. de Leon has earned his new position.

For Carlos, however, from a culture where status is more ascribed, Julie's questions aren't making any sense. Dr. de Leon's qualifications for the CEO position are not primarily a function of what he has done but of his social and economic standing, the family he was born into, and the people he knows. You don't necessarily earn status in such societies; you either have it or you don't. You may be able to add to it, of course, or to lose some of it, but a certain amount of status adheres to you based on accidents of birth. Indeed, it's not so much that this position confers status on Dr. de Leon, but that he brings his status to the position.

This is a classic distinction between a meritocracy and an aristocracy. In the former, you get the status in life that you have worked for; in the latter, you work to deserve the status you have been given.

The Cross-Cultural Perspective

In doing the exercises in this workbook, you have no doubt come to some realizations about your own culture and the cultures of certain other people about whom you wanted or needed to learn more. You will probably have discovered significant differences between yourself and some of these other people—different ways of behaving, different ways of thinking, perhaps even entirely different concepts of reality.

In short, chances are good that you will have come face-to-face with an important insight: that what you think of as right, normal, natural, and good may be very different from what some other people think. While you may still be toying with and inspecting this realization, not altogether sure what to make of it, you nevertheless now possess the beginnings of what we might call the cross-cultural perspective: the ability to interpret the behaviors of other people not from your own point of view, but from theirs.

This final chapter takes a brief look at this perspective, first with a quick test of your skills in this regard and then with a consideration of how you came by this cross-cultural perspective and where it will lead you. The idea here is that you have been changed by working through this book, and before you set it aside, you might want to reflect for a moment on just *how* you are different.

Chapter 5

To have your eyes widened and your organ of belief stretched, whilst remaining discreetly submissive, seems to me a faculty the tourist ought to cultivate. When you have submitted to looking about you discreetly and to observing with as little prejudice as possible, then you are in a proper state of mind to walk about...and learn from what you see.
—Philip Glazebrook
Journey to Kars

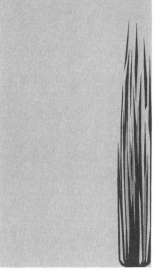

Exercise 5.1

Description or Interpretation?

Europeans will often show themselves willing to be what seems to [Americans] as subservient and even craven. For them, rank is right and helps give order to the world, in business as in the family and government.

—Stuart Miller
Understanding Europeans

As you have come to appreciate in this workbook, it's always safer in any kind of cross-cultural situation to describe behavior than to interpret it, at least initially. Interpreting behavior, after all, involves assigning meaning, and the meaning you assign to a behavior is bound to be one taken from your own culture—which won't necessarily help you very much if the person exhibiting the behavior comes from a different culture.

As far as possible, then, you should cultivate the ability to avoid interpreting behavior until such time as you can find out what the behavior in question means in the culture of the person exhibiting it. Meanwhile, you can develop the ability to describe behavior, to note the physical elements of a given act or set of acts without assigning meaning.

Eventually, of course, you have to assign meaning to behavior; you can't go around refusing to decide what people mean by the things they say and do. But by taking a moment to describe behavior before interpreting it, by holding in check the instinct to interpret, you can step back and realize you may be about to make a mistake.

Below, you will find ten pairs of statements; in each case, one is a description and one is an interpretation. Put a *D* next to the description and an *I* next to the interpretation.

_____ 1a. That man is very angry.

_____ 1b. That man is talking quite loudly.

_____ 2a. My boss doesn't trust his subordinates.

_____ 2b. My boss doesn't delegate responsibility.

_____ 3a. That woman stands three feet away when she speaks to me.

_____ 3b. That woman is cold and reserved.

_____ 4a. That man is afraid of his boss.

_____ 4b. That man never contradicts his boss in public.

_____ 5a. She doesn't have strong opinions.

_____ 5b. She never speaks up in meetings.

_____ 6a. That worker never does anything until he is told.

_____ 6b. That worker is lazy.

_____ 7a. He lied to me.

_____ 7b. He said yes when the answer to my question was no.

_____ 8a. She wasn't listening to me.

_____ 8b. She didn't look me in the eye when I was talking to her.

_____ 9a. He stood very close and gestured a lot when talking to me.

_____ 9b. He's very aggressive.

_____ 10a. She's insecure and power hungry.

_____ 10b. She doesn't share information with her subordinates.

Suggested Answers

_I_ 1a.
_D_ 1b.
_I_ 2a.
_D_ 2b.
_D_ 3a.
_I_ 3b.
_I_ 4a.
_D_ 4b.
_I_ 5a.
_D_ 5b.
_D_ 6a.
_I_ 6b.
_I_ 7a.
_D_ 7b.
_I_ 8a.
_D_ 8b.
_D_ 9a.
_I_ 9b.
_I_ 10a.
_D_ 10b.

The Stages of Cultural Awareness

The final exercise in the workbook examines the stages people go through in developing a cross-cultural perspective. You will now be fully engaged in this process yourself, having completed many or all of the previous exercises. Look at the four stages described below and then complete the exercise which follows.

1. *Unconscious Incompetence (blissful ignorance):* At this stage, you are not aware that there are cultural differences between people (or between you and a certain person); hence, it does not occur to you that you may be making cultural mistakes or that you may be misinterpreting much of the behavior going on around you. You have no reason at this stage not to trust your intuition.

2. *Conscious Incompetence (troubling ignorance):* You now realize that there are differences between the way you and people from other cultures behave, though you understand very little about just what these differences are, how numerous they might be, or how deep they might go. You know there's a problem here, in other words, but you're not sure of the size of it. You're not so sure of your intuition anymore, and you realize there are some things you don't understand. You may be worried at this stage about whether you'll ever be able to figure foreigners out.

3. *Conscious Competence (deliberate sensitivity):* You know there are cultural differences between people, you know what some of these differences are, and you try to modify your own behavior to be sensitive to these differences. All this doesn't come naturally yet—you have to make a conscious effort to behave in culturally sensitive ways—but you are much more aware of how your behavior is being interpreted by other people. You are in the process of re-

I've been asked if I live in a hut or a cave, or if I ever wore a shirt before coming to the U.S. When asked where I lived, I replied, "At the top of a tall tree."
"And how do you get there?"
"We use elevators."
—Ethiopian student in
John Fieg and John Blair
There Is a Difference

placing old intuitions with new ones. You know now that you will be able to figure these foreigners out if you can remain objective.

4. *Unconscious Competence (spontaneous sensitivity):* You no longer have to think about what you're doing in order to be culturally sensitive (in a culture you know well, that is, though not, of course, in one that is new to you). Culturally appropriate behavior comes naturally to you, and you can trust your intuition because it has been reconditioned by what you now know about cross-cultural interactions.

The exercise below requires you to think in some detail about these four stages. You will find eleven statements, each of which you are to assign to the stage of awareness you think the person who made this observation is in. Some of the statements could possibly go in more than one stage (but not more than two). Write the number of the stage (1, 2, 3, 4) in the blank preceding the observation.

_____ 1. I understand less than I thought I did.

_____ 2. These people ("foreigners" you have contact with) really aren't so different.

_____ 3. There is a logic to how these people behave.

_____ 4. Working with these people is like walking on eggshells.

_____ 5. These people have no trouble understanding me.

_____ 6. It's possible to figure these people out if you work at it.

_____ 7. I wonder what they think of me.

_____ 8. I know what they think of me.

_____ 9. It's nice to be able to relax and be myself around these people.

_____ 10. I'll never figure these people out.

_____ 11. Why did people say working with foreigners would be so difficult?

Suggested Answers

2 or 3 1. I understand less than I thought I did.

The better choice here is 2, for by the time you are in 3, you begin to understand more than you thought you did.

1 2. These people really aren't so different.

The only choice here is 1. If you were tempted to put 4, resist. Someone in 4 may understand foreigners very well and interact easily with them, but he/she knows quite well that these people are indeed very different.

3 3. There is a logic to how these people behave.

The best here is 3, for by now you are not only aware that these people are different (2), but you understand how they are different.

2 or 3 4. Working with these people is like walking on egg-shells.

The best answer is probably 2, for it is now beginning to dawn on you how easy it is to make mistakes. Someone in 3 might feel this way too, but by then you are starting to have more hope of figuring people out and avoiding mistakes.

1 5. These people have no trouble understanding me.

You might have put 4, but someone in 4, while he or she might find it easy to understand foreigners, would not assume that foreigners would find it easy to understand him or her.

3 6. It's possible to figure these people out if you work at it.

This is really the only choice here, for someone in 2 wouldn't necessarily know enough to know this yet.

5.2

2 or 3 7. I wonder what they think of me.

Stage 1 is out here, for such people think they know what other people think of them, and 4 is also out, because stage 4 people do know what other people are thinking. In 2 you would start to wonder this, and you could still be wondering in 3 as well, even as you are getting a grip on the culture.

1 or 4 8. I know what they think of me.

Those in 1 believe this mistakenly (because they think foreigners are just like other people, hence that they know what those from other cultures are thinking), but people in 4 believe this legitimately.

1 or 4 9. It's nice to be able to relax and be myself around these people.

People in 1 relax because they (wrongly) see nothing to worry about. People in 4 can relax and be themselves because they have acquired enough of the right instincts to be able to trust their behavior.

2 10. I'll never figure these people out.

This can only be 2, for by 3 you are beginning to figure people out.

1 11. Why did people say working with foreigners would be so difficult?

Because it is!

Epilogue

What you have learned from this workbook will depend in large part on what you knew when you started. But whatever your starting point, chances are you no longer see people from other cultures quite the way you did when you first picked up this volume. Among other things, you now realize that when you and they look at the world, you each see a different place. Some of their truths are not yours, and vice versa, and yet they are as sure of their verities as you are sure of yours. You are beginning to understand how it can happen that behavior which makes no sense to you, which may even offend you, could in fact be entirely logical and not at all offensive to someone from a different culture and quite possibly not meant the way you have taken it.

At the same time, you may also have grasped that when these same people look at you, they don't necessarily see what you think they see. They certainly don't see you the way you're used to being seen, by people from your own culture, that is, who see more or less a reflection of themselves. And they may not always understand your behavior the way you mean it—if they understand it at all. You now know, in short, that in communicating across the cultural divide you can't always be sure you're receiving the messages that are being sent, or that the messages you're sending are the ones being received.

There's no reason, by the way, why any of this should upset or discourage you. Yes, it may be rougher going at times in a multicultural world than in a monocultural one, but isn't it better, all and all, to see the world the way it is? It may be comforting to believe that other people are basically just like you, but it's neither wise nor safe. And what if this discovery does mean you may have to be more sensitive and self-aware than you're used to? Surely the world will somehow cope with an unexpected surge in sensitivity and self-awareness.

All good people agree,
And all good people say,
All nice people, like us,
* are We*
And everyone else is They.
But if you cross over the
* sea,*
Instead of over the way,
You may end by (think of
* it!) looking on We*
As only a sort of They!
* —Rudyard Kipling*
* "We and They"*

Recommended Reading

Readers interested in learning more about the topics presented in this guide should find the following books to their liking.

General

Axtell, Roger. *Gestures: Do's and Taboos of Body Language around the World*. New York: Wiley, 1991.

———. *Do's and Taboos around the World*. New York: Wiley, 1986.

Condon, John, and Fathi Yousef. *An Introduction to Intercultural Communication*. New York: Macmillan, 1975.

Fisher, Glen. *Mindsets: The Role of Culture and Perception in International Relations*. 2d ed. Yarmouth, ME: Intercultural Press, 1997.

Hall, Edward T. *The Dance of Life*. New York: Anchor/Doubleday, 1983.

———. *Beyond Culture*. 1976. Reprint, New York: Anchor/Doubleday, 1981.

———. *The Hidden Dimension*. 1966. Reprint, New York: Anchor/Doubleday, 1969.

———. *The Silent Language*. 1959. Reprint, New York: Anchor/Doubleday, 1973.

Hofstede, Geert. *Cultures and Organizations: Software of the Mind*. NY: McGraw-Hill, 1997.

———. *Culture's Consequences: International Differences in Work-Related Values*. Beverly Hills: Sage, 1980.

Samovar, Larry A., and Richard E. Porter, eds. *Intercultural Communication: A Reader*. 8th ed. Belmont, CA: Wadsworth, 1997.

Stewart, Edward C., and Milton J. Bennett. *American Cultural Patterns: A Cross-Cultural Perspective*. Rev. ed. Yarmouth, ME: Intercultural Press, 1991.

Storti, Craig. *Cross-Cultural Dialogues: 74 Brief Encounters with Cultural Difference*. Yarmouth, ME: Intercultural Press, 1994.

Business and the Workplace

Adler, Nancy. *International Dimensions of Organizational Behavior*. Boston: Kent, 1986.

Brake, Terence, et al. *Doing Business Internationally: The Guide to Cross-Cultural Success*. Princeton, NJ: Princeton Training Press, 1994.

Ferraro, Gary. *The Cultural Dimension of International Business*. 3d ed. Upper Saddle River, NJ: Prentice-Hall, 1998.

Foster, Dean Allen. *Bargaining across Borders*. New York: McGraw-Hill, 1992.

Hampden-Turner, Charles, and Alfons Trompenaars. *The Seven Cultures of Capitalism*. New York: Doubleday Currency, 1993.

Harris, Philip, and Robert T. Moran. *Managing Cultural Differences*. 4th ed. Houston: Gulf, 1996.

Harrison, Lawrence. *Who Prospers: How Cultural Values Shape Economic and Political Success*. New York: Basic Books, 1992.

Hickson, David, and Derek Pugh. *Management Worldwide*. London: Penguin Books, 1995.

Lane, Henry W., and Joseph DiStefano. *International Management Behavior*. Boston: Wadsworth, 1992.

Moran, Robert T., and William Stripp. *Dynamics of Successful International Business Negotiations*. Houston: Gulf, 1991.

Morrison, Terri, George A. Borden, and Wayne A. Conaway. *Kiss, Bow or Shake Hands: How to Do Business in Sixty Countries*. Holbrook, MA: Adams Media, 1994.

Phillips, Nicola. *Managing International Teams*. New York: Irwin, 1994.

Seelye, H. Ned, and Alan Seelye-Jones. *Culture Clash: Managing in a Multicultural World*. Lincolnwood, IL: NTC, 1995.

Trompenaars, Alfons. *Riding the Waves of Culture*. Chicago: Irwin Professional, 1994.

Wiseman, Richard, and Robert Shuter. *Communicating in Multinational Organizations*. Thousand Oaks, CA: Sage, 1994.

Geographic Regions

Cavusgil, S. Tamer. *Doing Business in Developing Countries: Entry and Negotiation Strategies*. London and New York: Routledge, 1990.

Devine, Elizabeth, and Nancy Braganti. *European Customs and Manners*. New York: Meadowbrook, 1992.

————. *The Traveler's Guide to Middle Eastern and North African Customs*. New York: St. Martin's Press, 1991.

————. *The Traveler's Guide to Latin American Customs and Manners*. New York: St. Martin's Press, 1988.

————. *The Traveler's Guide to Asian Customs and Manners*. New York: St. Martin's Press, 1986.

Dunung, Sanjyot P. *Doing Business in Asia: The Complete Guide*. New York: Lexington Books, 1995.

Engholm, Christopher. *When Business East Meets Business West*. New York: John Wiley & Sons, 1991.

Gannon, Martin J. *Understanding Global Cultures: Metaphorical Journeys through Seventeen Countries*. Thousand Oaks, CA: Sage, 1994.

Hall, Edward T., and Mildred Reed Hall. *Understanding Cultural Differences: Germans, French and Americans*. Yarmouth, ME: Intercultural Press, 1989.

Hill, Richard. *We Europeans*. 3d ed. Brussels: Europublications, 1995.

————. *Euromanagers and Martians: The Business Cultures of Europe's Trading Nations*. Brussels: Europublications, 1994.

Lewis, Richard. *When Cultures Collide*. London: Nicolas Brealey, 1996.

Mole, John. *Mind Your Manners: Managing Business Cultures in Europe*. London: Nicholas Brealey, 1995.

Moran, Robert T. *Cultural Guide to Doing Business in Europe*. Oxford and Boston: Butterworth-Heinemann, 1992.

The Expatriate Experience

Black, J. Stewart, Hal B. Gregerson, and Mark E. Mendenhall. *Global Assignments: Successfully Expatriating and Repatriating International Managers*. San Francisco: Jossey-Bass, 1992.

Kohls, L. Robert. *Survival Kit for Overseas Living: For Americans Planning to Live and Work Abroad*. 3d ed. Yarmouth, ME: Intercultural Press, 1996.

Osland, Joyce Sautters. *The Adventure of Working Abroad*. San Francisco: Jossey-Bass, 1995.

Pascoe, Robin. *Culture Shock: A Parent's Guide*. Singapore: Times Editions, 1993.

———. *Surviving Overseas: The Wife's Guide to Successful Living Abroad*. Singapore: Times Editions, 1992.

Piet-Pelon, Nancy J., and Barbara Hornby. *Women's Guide to Overseas Living*. 2d ed. Yarmouth, ME: Intercultural Press, 1992.

Shames, Germaine. *Transcultural Odysseys: The Evolving Global Consciousness*. Yarmouth, ME: Intercultural Press, 1997.

Storti, Craig. *The Art of Coming Home*. Yarmouth, ME: Intercultural Press, 1997.

———. *The Art of Crossing Cultures*. Yarmouth, ME: Intercultural Press, 1990.

Individual Countries

For information about specific countries, the following series are recommended. There are a number of titles in each series, with each title covering one country. Note that the focus in these books is on culture in the way it has been used in this workbook, that is, having to do with behaviors, norms, values, and beliefs. The books in these series have very little country information (about history, geography, politics, or economics), nor are they guidebooks.

The Interact Series:

Intercultural Press
P.O. Box 700
Yarmouth, ME 04096 USA
866-372-2665
207-846-5168
e-mail:
books@interculturalpress.com
www.interculturalpress.com

The Culture Shock Series:

Graphic Arts Center
 Publishing Co.
P.O. Box 10306
Portland, OR 97296 USA
503-226-2402

Passport to the World:

World Trade Press
1450 Grant Avenue, Suite 204
Novato, CA 94945 USA
415-454-9934
e-mail:
sales@worldtradepress.com